CHAN
IS
MISSING

a film by Wayne Wang

with introduction and screen notes by Diane Mei Lin Mark

Bamboo Ridge Press

1984

Library of Congress Catalog Card Number: 83-73233
ISBN 0-910043-06-X

Copyright 1984 by Wayne Wang Productions, Inc.
Introduction, screen notes and interview copyright 1984 by Diane
Mei Lin Mark.
Published by Bamboo Ridge Press and the Hawaii Ethnic
Resources Center: Talk Story, Inc.
Cover and book design: Phyllis Y. Miyamoto

For information regarding the availability of *Chan Is Missing*, please
call or write:

New Yorker Films
16 West 61st Street
New York, New York 10023
(212) 247-6110

This project was supported by a grant from the National
Endowment for the Arts (NEA) in Washington, D.C., a federal
agency.

Bamboo Ridge Press
P.O. Box 61781
Honolulu, Hawaii 96839-1781
(808) 599-4823

10 9 8 7 6 5 4 3

Acknowledgments

Mahalo nui loa to all those who helped in the translation of "Chan is Missing" from film to paper. Bev Lum was instrumental in the initial connecting of principal parties. Wing Tek Lum helped in both an advisory capacity and in the transcription and translation of the Chinese sections of the screenplay. He was assisted by Chee Ping Lee Lum and Chien Chang. The Chinese type was set in Hong Kong by Goldwind Photo Typesetting Co., with the assistance of Dr. Sin-wai Chan.

Bamboo Ridge editors Darrell Lum and Eric Chock gave us moral support and artistic latitude. Alice Matsumoto transcribed the English dialogue, was briefly interrupted by the birth of her baby(!), then typeset the final manuscript. Many hours of reviewing the film were logged on the video equipment of Susan Pang, who also programmed her word processor to expedite our compilation of reviews.

Last but not least, special thanks to Wayne Wang for his assistance in the preparation of the materials which follow, and, in a most basic sense, for making this volume possible.

Diane Mark

Table of Contents

Introduction

We're sitting in the dark, tapping our toes to the driving beat of "Rock Around the Clock," Hong Kong style. The images start. What looks like a white screen is actually a windshield reflecting sky. It begins to fill with environmental reflections as the car moves down the street. For a brief moment we see Jo, the driver. The glass whites out again with passing sky, followed by more reflections. A glimpse of hand on wheel. We are working hard, involved, trying to keep up with the changing portrait. And the opening credits are still rolling.

This is the tone-setting first scene of the feature film "Chan is Missing," by producer/director Wayne Wang. Suspense and comedy work on one level, but a dash of social comment is subtly evident as well. The reflections which move quickly across the windshield are views of San Francisco Chinatown as well as precursors of a theme which unfolds during the course of the film, regarding the interpretation of reality.

"Chan is Missing" follows two San Francisco Chinatown cabbies in their search for Chan Hung, a missing partner who is in possession of $4,000 of their money. The film is at once a spoof on the Charlie Chan genre and a statement on Chinese America in a diversity hitherto undepicted in theatrical film history. As the two cabbies, Jo (Wood Moy) and Steve (Marc Hayashi) comb Chinatown for clues leading to their partner, they encounter a full range of characters in the community, each imbued with a unique personality, each sharing a different impression of the increasingly enigmatic Chan. There is Henry the wok cook (Peter Wang), who guzzles milk and is tired of cooking sweet-and-sour pork for white folks. There is a young Asian American woman lawyer (Judy Nihei), whose fast, circular talk on Chinese-English semantics is an exercise in semantics itself. There is Chan's estranged wife (Ellen Yeung), who is trying to make a go of it in America and feels her husband is "too Chinese" to do likewise. There is Mr. Lee (Roy Chan), Chan's sponsor and insurance man, who regards Chan as an immigrant who needs educating. There is Mr. Fong (Leung Pui Chee), a scholar who thinks the key to finding Chan Hung is to "think Chinese."

The film's central characters, Jo and Steve, are both ABC (American-born Chinese) in contrast to Chan, who is FOB (fresh off the boat). But because Jo is second generation, one generation closer to the immigration experience (Steve is third), he empathizes with Chan Hung, especially when Steve accuses Chan of absconding with their money. The major conflict between Jo and Steve is a heated argument which erupts on the pier after several days of unsuccessful searching. Jo defends Chan's integrity; Steve questions it. If Chan is a metaphor for Chinatown, or the "Chinese" part of Chinese American identity, then Jo's defense of Chan and his dogged attempt to find him is symbolic of the second generation's relative loyalty to Chinese culture, especially in discussions with the young. Likewise, Steve's distance from Chan, his feeling of having been cheated by him, his inability to understand why Jo trusts him, is representative of a Chinese American who has found little use for Chinese thought and culture for his survival in the United States.

This very presentation of diversity among Chinese American characters in a film is a concept largely untested in American movies. Mainstream viewers have previously been exposed to a mere handful of Chinese character types recycled over and over again. Stereotypic portrayals have been the rule. Wang replaces these stock images with realistic, everyday characters who bear little resemblance to each other or to their predecessors in western film history.

Hollywood Images

In theatrical history, "Chan is Missing" can easily be considered a breakthrough film. It stands out in its depiction of Asian Americans as people (versus props), 3-D (versus 1- and 2-), and self-expressive (versus deaf-mute or programmed with Confucianisms). During the silent film era, such hits as "The Chinese Rubbernecks" (1903), "Heathen Chinese and The Sunday School Teacher" (1904), and "The Yellow Peril" (1908) reinforced what most Americans suspected—that Chinese were alien, cunning, and somewhat laughable.

Always the pioneer, D.W. Griffith, in "Broken Blossoms" (1919), established, unwittingly perhaps, several stylistic elements in the characterization of Chinese which have been repeated in film to this day. One element was the use of white actors in yellow face to fill Asian roles. In the PEARLS documentary "Mako" (Educational Film Center, 1979), a makeup artist demonstrates how Hollywood still achieves that slant-eyed, buck-toothed "Asian look" today.

The most well-known Asian characters in American film history have been portrayed by white actors and actresses. The list is lengthy. To appear Asian, these actors and actresses adopted exaggerated mannerisms which, repeatedly done, created stereotypes and cardboard caricatures. Actors Warner Oland and Boris Karloff played Fu Manchu for a successive four decades. Peter Sellers revived the character in 1980. Warner Oland transferred his acting-Asian skills to the portrayal of Charlie Chan, a role later played by Sidney Toler and Roland Winters, and in 1980, by Peter Ustinov. In television, David Carradine was cast in the "Kung Fu" series, playing a Shaolin monk wandering, dazed, through the Wild West.

Another element retained from the days of Griffith is the negative resolution of white-Asian love relationships. The Asian male's threat to white womanhood (read "white manhood") is usually eradicated by the end of the film, through the death or departure of the Asian man. A third element which has persisted to shape the image of Asians on film is the vision of Chinatown as a mysterious, quaint, exotic place. The dark, dank streets of Griffith's Chinatown echo in many contemporary Hollywood movies and television dramas.

These and other film images of Asians in America have occurred and reoccurred throughout the century. Because of the larger-than-life influence of the screen, these Asian stereotypes reinforce impressions and, in young minds, give root. But the stock roles are reflective of societal mores and perceptions, and thus are not adverse to box-office sales. And so the images persist.

Asian American Filmmaking

As influenced by the civil rights and Black movements of the 1960s, the Asian American movement precipitated not only political change, but a cultural renaissance. In this unique historical period, there was the highly-motivated creation of poetry, drama, short stories, novels, music, video and films which were expressly "Asian American." Most of this work by Asian American creative artists has over the ensuing decade and a half been enjoyed within the community alone. A non-exotic Chinatown does not a Hollywood hit make.

In the area of film and video, Visual Communications (Los

Angeles) produced numerous documentaries (e.g., "Wataridori: Birds of Passage," "Cruisin' J-town," "Chinatown 2-Step") and a first Asian American dramatic feature film, "Hito Hata: Raise the Banner." Christine Choy (Third World Newsreel, New York) made a number of documentaries, including "From Spikes to Spindles," "Bittersweet Survival" (with J.T. Takagi), and "Mississippi Chinese." For the past six years, the "best of" Asian and Asian American films has been rounded up for the Asian American International Film Festival, sponsored by the media arts organization Asian CineVision in New York City. A few film series have been produced for television and broadcast on PBS. The Educational Film Center (Springfield, Va.) sponsored the production of the first two Asian American film series aired nationally on public television, "Pacific Bridges" and "Pearls" (executive producer Noel Izon). San Francisco producer Loni Ding featured community children in the series "Bean Sprouts." In fall 1983, "Silkscreen," a collection of Asian American films by independent producers (packaged by the National Asian American Telecommunications Association) was aired for a national audience on PBS.

While exposure of Asian American productions has been gradually improving in the realm of television, this has not been true in the theatrical marketplace. "Chan is Missing" was the first Asian American film to "cross over" and enjoy success in the mainstream film world. It received its major boost in the New Directors/New Films Film Festival at the Museum of Modern Art, New York, accompanied by an enthusiastic review by *New York Times* film critic Vincent Canby, who called the film a "matchless delight" and the "revelation of a marvelous, secure new talent." "Not since the final frames of Louis Bunuel's 'Tristana,'" wrote Canby, "has there been an ending so dazzling in its utter simplicity." *The Village Voice*'s Carrie Ricky wrote, "Wang has composed a valentine, not a dirge, for the collision of cultures." Movie reviewers around the country sent equal praise to press. Most were amazed at how skillfully the production's meager $20,000 budget had been used. Towards the end of this deluge of hosannas, however, some critics stressed that this was, after all, a $20,000 film, with all its inherent limitations, and that the excess raving was placing undue pressure on this new director's future. What stands out in the mass of reviews of "Chan is Missing" is the critic's joyful message that good 1980s filmmaking is not just multi-million dollar budgets, bankable stars, and special effects. The basis for a good film is still a good story.

Box Office Success
There are several key elements which stand out in an examination of the box office success of "Chan is Missing." Most basic is the competence of the production itself, traceable to the talents of a largely Asian American cast and crew, as orchestrated by producer/director Wang. Assisted by writer Terrel Seltzer, Wang developed a dramatic framework which left room for additional input and on-location improvisation by the principal cast. The other writer credited, Isaac Cronin, developed voice-over narration.

Actors Wood Moy and Marc Hayashi played important roles not only in the film itself, but in the synergistic process of fleshing out the drama, based on their senses of character and plot action. In supporting character roles, Judy Nihei, Peter Wang, Roy Chan, and George Woo deserve special mention. Musical selection and composition by Robert Kikuchi-Yngonjo effectively strengthens the film's visual concepts. The mixture of Hong Kong pop, Pat Suzuki ("Grant Avenue"), and Kikuchi-Yngonjo's own Asian American music not only enhances the drama but is reflective of the diverse nature of Chinatown life. Cinematographer Michael Chin worked well in the documentary-type shoot-from-the-hip format. His montages of Chinatown scenes contain numerous well-composed shots which document both the minute and broad aspects of the community canvas.

A second key element in the successful reception of "Chan is Missing" is the time of its release. The stage was set by a progression of events which began, in one sense, with the Asian American movement of the late 1960s, during which there emerged in the Asian American community the desire to create alternatives to Charlie Chan, Fu Manchu, Suzie Wong, and other stock portrayals of Asians. Wayne Wang's own sensibility of Asian America began to take shape when he was a San Francisco Bay Area college student during this turning point in Asian American history.

"Chan is Missing," like other successes, might well be viewed in the context of the cultural developments which influenced its creation. A body of Asian American works in theater, film, and literature was steadily produced within the national Asian community, building in quality and sophistication through the 1970s. Much of this work was not afforded dissemination by mainstream publishers and producers, whose decisions are based primarily on financial viability and current trends in the marketplace. In the mid- and late-1970s, Maxine Hong Kingston and David Henry Hwang received broad public attention in the worlds of literature and theater.

This exposure of Asian American subject matter on the best seller and hit play lists, despite controversy in the Asian American arts community, furthered the concept of Asian American culture in the public mind. All these factors readied the stage for a "Chan is Missing" to appear in the film world, and garner success from general audiences.

Thirdly, the popularity of "Chan is Missing" might be traced to its offering of a slice of American life which is unique and new, a characteristic looked upon with particular favor by the cinematically-sophisticated moviegoers of the 1980s. Wang's Chinatown is inside—inside the Chinese restaurant, inside the kitchen, inside the wok. It is inside family apartments, cafes, and even inside Jo's head. In his documentary-type treatment of this traditionally exotic locale, Wang manages to simultaneously satisfy both the white mainstream audience, which has never had this first-hand filmic experience, and Asian American viewers, who find a realistic portrait of themselves a refeshing relief.

"Chan" As A Film

"Chan is Missing" is not without its problems as a film. The marriage of documentary and dramatic formats works more successfully in some scenes than others. The use of professional amidst non-professional actors and actresses somewhat affects the evenness of tone throughout the film. The film's low budget is also evidenced in its simplified, sometimes repetitive camera technique, including static shots, numerous close-ups of news clippings and the "flag-waving incident" photograph, and borderline talking head shots which afford characters little movement but are economical in terms of production. There are also numerous "thinking head" shots—Jo alone in thought at a table, in his cab, walking down the street, with voice-over narration. But Wang has found ways to make these difficulties work in favor of the film. The hand-held shots, for example, actually provide an intimacy that further pulls us into the film, giving us the sense of going along on the hunt for Chan. The hand-held and from-the-car shots liberate the camera, infusing it with the same freedom enjoyed by Steve and Jo as they move at will through Chinatown. We also slip briefly into the skins of characters for which the camera takes the point-of-view, including a waiter serving a table and the grandmother who intently watches a scene from an upstairs window and feigns indifference when the action enters the room.

In the past, Asian American plays and films have concentrated on soul-searching, lessons of history, examination of the

Asian-white relationships, generational conflict—very serious subjects which have been treated as such. In recent years, the plays of David Henry Hwang ("FOB," "Family Devotions") and Rick Shiomi ("Yellow Fever") have upped the "entertainment quotient" of Asian American theatrical drama. "Chan is Missing" shares their ability to make people laugh along with, rather than at, Asian characters. "Chan" also operates with the awareness of general audiences, injecting the added dimension of genuine affection for the community.

With decades of demeaning portrayals of Asians in film and television, the tendency for contemporary Asian American filmmakers has been to earnestly counterbalance Asian media images by creating ultra-positive characters. Character faults are attributed less to individual deficiencies and inabilities than to the binds of history, racism, and tradition. In "Chan is Missing," the characters are everyday people who don't always keep their cool, stay on top of the situation, or find what they are looking for. Wang's characterizations show Asian Americans as human beings rather than dime-a-dozen stereotypes or do-no-wrong heroes, typical characterizations which are equally dehumanizing on either end of the scale. "Chan is Missing" has demonstrated that it might not be necessary for Asians to kowtow, cater, or conquer through jeet kune do to assure box office viability.

As viewers, we are also offered a language lesson while watching this film. Ears are initiated to Cantonese and Mandarin, in addition to Chinese American English in Black dialect, professional dialect, Chinatown dialect, wok cook dialect. And if language is a medium of culture, then we are brought to a closer understanding of the societal variety of Chinese Americans and their tendency to not all look (and talk) alike.

"Chan is Missing" might, in addition, provoke more troubling thoughts about Chinese American society. There is the notion of the disintegration of the Chinese American family. Jo is divorced and the Chans are estranged. For a people traditionally touted to have overriding family ties and the unerring ability to take care of their own, this is a divergence. There is also the portrayal of Chinatown as one which is filled with complexity, even for Chinese Americans. We are shown a Chinatown which is a living, breathing community filled with optimism and dashed dreams, the daily grind and political intrigue. Chan is missing. If Chan symbolizes the Chinese part of Chinese America, the question is, should the search continue, and are we prepared for the find?

Changing Perceptions
The artistry of a film piece made within a genre can be
measured by the filmmaker's original contributions to the
established conventions and his/her ability to absorb and
react to its standard features to give a unique expression to
the form. Within the mystery genre, Wang utilizes various
conventions—the disappearance, the chase scene, the
pounding suspense music. He refuses, however, to exploit
Chinatown by presenting it as the exotic, dark, mysterious
locale it has traditionally been used for in the genre. "Chan is
Missing" depicts everyday life on Chinatown streets and
within its offices, businesses, and homes. But the difference
between the real and the heretofore reel Chinatown has been
so great that the effect is far from mundane.

In another original take to the mystery genre tradition,
Wang does away with the normal ending to the story. The
Western-created Charlie Chan would have solved the puzzle.
Jo and Steve, for all their efforts, do not. This has, in fact,
been one of the criticisms of "Chan is Missing." The lack of a
traditional resolution to the mystery has been unfortunately
interpreted as a lack of resolution altogether. But the notion
that Wang has suggested throughout the film—the Asian
ability to search hard for a solution while accepting ambiguity
—is underscored in this ending, which is, in fact, the only
ending possible.

A primary vehicle for this inherent ambiguity is the use of
the "negative" character. One of the most successful sequences
in the film is one in which Jo walks and drives through the
Chinatown streets with the fear that he is being followed.
With gripping music and a series of quick cuts—a glance in
the rearview mirror, a close-up of feet walking, a look over the
shoulder directly into the camera—Wang has constructed a
suspenseful chase scene in which the camera perspective is
that of the pursuer. This pursuer, whether a figment of Jo's
imagination or a real person, is, like Chan Hung, a "negative"
character whose presence is felt but not seen.

As in most movies, "Chan is Missing" ends with a with-
drawal, in this case, of camera from locale. The final sequence
of scenes commences with a shot of Steve and Jo relaxing in
their cab, which is parked beneath the Golden Gate Bridge,
away from Chinatown. They no longer talk directly about
Chan Hung, but reflect on the merits and contradictions of
"thinking Chinese." The segue to the ending montage is a
long hold on a shot of rippling Bay water reflecting the sunlight. By its reversible, flat nature, it is a scene wide open to
interpretation, and perhaps a most appropriate cinematic met-

aphor for the entire film. As volume is pulled up on the music track, we hear Pat Suzuki belting out "Grant Avenue, San Francisco, California, U.S.A...." and are left with a punctuated sense of the vast differences between tinseled storefronts and real people in movement on the streets of their community.

Diane Mark

Credits

Produced and directed by .... Wayne Wang
Written by .... Wayne Wang
Isaac Cronin
Terrel Seltzer
Cameraman .... Michael Chin
Editor .... Wayne Wang
Soundman .... Curtis Choy
Music... Robert Kikuchi
Chinese Pop Music................................Sam Hui
Courtesy of Polydor Records, Hong Kong
Production Manager .... Sara Chin
Continuity ....Piera Kwan
Production assistants .... Julian Low
Don Wong
Bob Yano

Produced with grants from the American Film Institute and the National Endowment for the Arts by Wayne Wang Productions, Inc.

Cast
(in order of appearance)

Jo .... Wood Moy
Steve .... Marc Hayashi
Amy... Laureen Chew
Lawyer .... Judi Nihei
Henry, the cook .... Peter Wang
Presco ....Presco Tabios
Frankie.................................... Frankie Alarcon
Mrs. Chan .... Ellen Yeung
Jenny .... Emily Yamasaki
George... George Woo
Jenny's friend .... Virginia Cerenio
Mr. Lee .... Roy Chan
Mr. Fong ....Leung Pui Chee

Chan Is Missing

This film is dedicated to:
WONG CHEEN

FADE IN
1. EXT. (Exterior scene) SAN FRANCISCO CHINATOWN—DAY

SFX (Sound effects): "Gà Ga Yiht Chïuh*," a Chinese pop song about inflation in Hong Kong set to the music of "Rock Around the Clock"

Environmental reflections change across the windshield of a moving car. JO, Chinese American, middle-aged, and low key, is at the wheel of his Wing On taxicab. We see him only intermittently, through the glass, as it reflects the Chinatownscape and whites out with passing sky.

> PASSENGER
> Hilton, please.

> JO (VO: Voiceover)
> There's a game I play. One thousand, two thousand, three thousand...

> PASSENGER
> Hey, uh, what's a good place to eat in Chinatown?

> JO (VO)
> Under three seconds. That question comes up under three seconds 90 percent of the time. I usually give them my routine on the differences between

*"Inflation Fever" 加價熱潮

Mandarin and Cantonese food
and get a *good* tip.

2. INT. (Interior scene) STEVE AND AMY'S APARTMENT—
EVENING

Jo enters the kitchen and is greeted by his nephew STEVE,
20s, fast-talking and street-wise; and Steve's sister AMY, older
20s, equally fast-talking, and adept at teasing. Steve and Amy
sit at the table eating dinner and Jo joins them.

STEVE
So what you doing. What are you
doing here? I thought you said
you weren't going to come.

AMY
Hey, who invited you?

JO
You invited me.

AMY
I didn't invite you.

STEVE
Hubba, hubba, hubba, hubba.

JO
How about a beer.

AMY
What about a beer? Go get it
yourself. You know where it is.
You've been here enough.

JO
I thought you guys weren't going
to eat at home.

STEVE
Yeah. I was going to take my
mother and sister out. We were
going to go to the Golden
Lantern. But see, all the people
there are from Taiwan, and Gum
Sing, you know, all the

Communists eat there, so we
decided to eat at home.

                AMY
And at home, we have this U.S.
certified food here, you know,
chicken, cow's ear, herb skunk.
Hey, eh, don't eat that much
(addresses Steve), you, that's
from China.

                STEVE
Hey, this is from Iowa, Des
Moines Iowa, man. Don't wave a
PRC flag around here, man.

                JO
What do you mean, PRC flag
around here?

                STEVE
(gets an idea and pretends to pose
        as a T.V. news reporter)
Eh, what kind of "Chinese"
Chinese are you? PRC? Huh?
Taiwan, Pro Taiwan? Richmond
district? Oakland hill, wa? Ho
Chi Minh, yeah,yeah.

                AMY
Oh, flags, talking about flags,
guess what happened?

                STEVE
You met the Flagg brothers.

                AMY
No. (laughs) Guess who called me
today?

                STEVE
Who called you?

                JO
Who? Who?

AMY
Gary. Remember Gary? He called
me five times.

STEVE
Oh, Gary Lai, the one with the
Porsche?

AMY
Yeah.

STEVE
I think he like you.

AMY
I wish he did. Anyway, Gary
called to tell me that he was...

STEVE
(Interjects)
Probably scare him away, you
know.

AMY
No, no, no. He told me he was
going to sue the city for the hotel
tax because he thought it was a
misuse of funds for the flag-
waving business. Gary is really
afraid of his Taiwan competitor
so he wants him to look bad. You
know the guy who's running for
Supervisor?

JO
Isn't Gary running with Taiwan
support?

STEVE
Nah, he jumped on the Commie
bandwagon, you know.

AMY
(Interrupts)
Commie bandwagon!!

STEVE
You know, the Commie with the
new Chinese money that's
coming in now. Yeah, he's a
Commie lover now.

JO
So who's running on the
Taiwan—

AMY
Oh, I know, I know. This guy
named Lee Kwock Wai.

AMY
Hey, guess what. This guy Paul's
running too. You know Paul, the
neuter candidate? I mean the
Chinese American candidate?
Remember him?

STEVE
You know what's going to
happen with all these guys.
Going like that (pushes fists
together). You know, the voters
are going to be herded in by all
those organizers, except they're
going to vote for that guy, Bernie
Lee, from the Castro district—
that gay candidate. And
Chinatown's gonna end up with
a gay Sup, you know.

AMY
Oh, that gay candidate? Oh,
they'd love it, everyone would
love it.

Jo rotates a toy on the table and points to it. It's a child's
piano labelled the Big Mouth Singers with a keyboard
connected to eight heads.

JO
What's that? Huh?

STEVE
Huh?

JO
Gógo a*—this.

STEVE
(imitates Jo speaking Chinese)
He's always doing that. Huh?
Huh? Wha—?

JO
Huh?

STEVE
What is it? Huh?

JO
Ho—

STEVE
Huh?

JO
Hah—

STEVE
My nephew's.

JO
Your nephew? What's your
nephew's?

STEVE
My nephew's piano.

Steve starts playing with the keys.

JO
Sounds just like you.

STEVE
St. Mary's. St. Mary's drill.

He pounds out a march tune.

3. EXT. STREET—DAY

Jo drives his taxi through traffic on the streets.

*That thing　嗰個呀

JO (VO)
Last week, my nephew Steve and
I decided to get a cab license so
we can be our own boss. We had
to sublease the license from an
independent owner in
Chinatown. My niece Amy and
my friend Chan Hung helped set
up the deal. The thing was that
Chan Hung had to take cash to
go finalize everything. Steve felt
uneasy about that, but Amy and
I convinced him that it would be
okay. But I'm a little worried
about Chan Hung. We haven't
seen him for two days. This
morning when Steve and I were
having breakfast at Chester's, a
woman showed up looking for
Chan Hung. It was about a car
accident he was in.

4. INT. CAFE—DAY

Jo and Steve sit at a table listening to a young Asian American woman lawyer. We cut back to their bemused looks as she
rambles on in professionalese.

LAWYER
You see, I'm doing a paper on the
legal implications of cross-cutural
misunderstandings, and Mr.
Chan's case is a perfect example
of what I'm trying to expose here.
You see, the policeman and Mr.
Chan had completely different
culturally-related assumptions
about what kind of communications about communication each
one was using. For instance, the
policeman in an English-
speaking mode asked a direct
factual question. They're
interested in facts and that's all.
Asked, "Did you stop at the stop
sign?"—expected a yes or no

answer. Simple yes or no answer.
Mr. Chan, however, rather than
giving him a yes or no answer,
began to go into his past driving
record, how good it was, the
number of years he'd been in the
States, all the people that he
knew, trying to relate different
events or objects or situations to
what was happening then, to the
action at hand. Now this is very
typical, as I'm sure you know, of
most Chinese speakers. Trying to
relate possibly unrelated objects
or seemingly unrelated objects to
the matter at hand. Chinese try
to relate points, or events, or
objects tuat they feel are
pertinent to the situation which
may not to anyone else seem
directly relevant at the time. At
any rate, at this the policeman
became rather impatient, restated
the question, "Did you or did you
not stop at the stop sign?" in a
rather hostile tone, which in turn,
flustered Mr. Chan, which caused
him to hesitate answering the
question, which further enraged
the policeman, so that he asked
the question again, "You didn't
stop at the stop sign, did you?" in
a negative tone, to which Mr.
Chan automatically answered,
"No." Now, to any native speaker
of English, "No" would mean,
"No, I didn't stop at the stop
sign." However, to Mr. Chan,
"No, I didn't stop at the stop
sign," wasn't "No, I didn't stop
at the stop sign." It was "No, I
didn't not stop at the stop sign,"
in other words, "Yes, I did stop at
the stop sign." You see what I'm
saying? He was, um, correct in
the Chinese because the answer

has to match the truth of the action. However, English speakers, native American English speakers, tend to work more from a grammatical mode. To put it in layman's language, English language emphasizes the relationship between grammatical structures and the Chinese language tends to emphasize the relationship between the listener, the speaker, and the action involved. Well, at any rate, Mr. Chan has to appear in court so we can get this all straightened out so we can explain everything, and he missed his court date.

                    STEVE
Wait, wait a minute. When does he have to appear in court?

                    LAWYER
Our court date was last week. That's why I'm trying to find him. He wasn't there last week, and—

                    STEVE
He didn't tell us about that.

                    LAWYER
Well have you seen him? Do you know where I can get a hold of him, because I've got to make another appointment. We've got to get—

5. INT. HOTEL ST. PAUL—DAY

Jo and Steve go to Chan Hung's hotel apartment to look for him.

                    JO (VO)
Chan Hung wouldn't run away because of the car accident. But I

have a strong feeling something
might have happened to him. We
decided to go look for him after
work. Chan Hung wasn't home.

6. INT. CAFE—DAY

Steve and Jo relax at a table, drinking beer.

> STEVE
> You know, I went down to the
> Great Star Theatre. Saw this
> Chinese version of Saturday
> Night Fever, you know, except
> the song, the beginning of the
> song went, "You can tell by the
> way I use my wok, I'm a Chinese
> cook, I'm a Chinese cook.
> (laughs) Hey, you want another
> beer?

7. INT. GOLDEN DRAGON RESTAURANT KITCHEN—DAY*

SFX: Henry the cook singing "Fry Me to the Moon"

Dressed in a Samurai Night Fever t-shirt, Henry, speaking
primarily in Mandarin, is busily reading orders, mixing
sauces, wok-frying, and guzzling milk.

> JO (VO)
> Steve's joke reminded me of
> someone Chan Hung talks about
> a lot. The cook at the Golden
> Dragon who wears a Samurai
> Night Fever t-shirt, drinks milk,
> chain smokes, and sings "Fry Me
> to the Moon," all while he's
> cooking up five orders of sweet
> and sour pork.

> HENRY
> ...shémma?

He picks up an order on a slip of paper.

*See pp. 79-85 for English translation and pp. 91-96 for Chinese character text for
this entire scene

Hē! Tyánswān páigú sànfén!
Tāmāde! Jèi Choùlǎu měi
yītyāndàuwǎn jyòu chī jèige. Wǒ
jèn bùdǔng. Shémma hǎuchīde
ma? Tyánswān páigú...Tāmāde!
Wǒ nàwèi swān...yòu lái le!

He drinks some milk.

Ou, tāmāde!

He takes another gulp.

Jèi chúfáng bùshī réngànde.
Wǒ gàusyǔ nǐ, nǐ titóu shīfù yě
wèi chyán, wéije yǐdz jwàn ywán
chwān. Dzámén lyóusywéshēng
dzémma yàng? Lyóusywéshēng
yě wèi chyán wéije hùolú wàn
gwōchǎn! Hāhā! Tāmāde!

CUT TO:

The dining room of the restaurant. Camera POV (point-of-
view) is that of a waiter taking orders from patrons. At one
table, an older Chinese couple and their daughter discuss their
choices, partly in Cantonese.

DAUGHTER
What about, what about a—
baahkchoi?

FATHER
Baahkchoi m̀hóu la. Chìngcháau
gaailàahn la, hóu ma?

MOTHER
Hóu ngahn...

DAUGHTER
No, I want something with beef
in it. (to CAM: camera) You have
something with beef in it?

MOTHER
Hóu fèih...

DAUGHTER
What about...

FATHER
Mngāam sïungáap lā, hóu ma?

MOTHER
Sïungáap fèih...sihk gài.

DAUGHTER
No, that's too heavy, that's too
heavy for lunch, mom...what
about fish?

FATHER
(tentatively)
Chïngjïng...chïngjïng...

DAUGHTER
Yeah, yeah...fish.

FATHER
...sehkbàan.

DAUGHTER
Yeah.

MOTHER
Òh, hóu a.

DAUGHTER
Yeah, that rock cod sounds good.

CUT TO:

Another table, where a young man hands back a dish of food
to the waiter.

YOUNG MAN (to CAM)
We didn't order this.

The young man shakes his head and turns to the young
woman next to him.

YOUNG WOMAN
...you know, did you see that
movie...

Jo and Steve enter through the front door of the restaurant
and speak to a waitress.

> WAITRESS
> He's working downstairs in the
> kitchen. You want to see him?

> JO
> Yeah... m̀gòi.

> WAITRESS
> Okay, you go here (pointing) and go
> down.

> JO
> Mgòi... m̀gòi...

Jo and Steve make their way through the dining room towards
the kitchen. We hear snatches of conversation between the
young man and woman.

> YOUNG WOMAN
> ...long time...

> YOUNG MAN
> ...long time ago...

> YOUNG WOMAN
> ...that's a good one... but
> another thing is a...

CUT TO:

Another table, occupied by a white man, a white woman, and
across the table two Chinese women, speaking partly in
Cantonese, who cannot be seen directly but only via a reflection in the mirror.

> CHINESE WOMAN
> ...jànhaih màhfàahn ga... m̀hóu
> góng... (referring to the white
> man) lauhhei gwái lèihga, néih
> jànhaih! (giggles)

> WHITE WOMAN
> (to white man) What's lauhhei?
> (turns to the Chinese woman)
> What's lauhhei?

24

WHITE MAN
(starts to explain)
Lauhhei...

SECOND CHINESE WOMAN
(squeals)
Leaking gas!

WHITE WOMAN
Leaking what?

WHITE MAN
Lauhhei means...(others are all
laughing)...not together, not
together; I didn't do it.

CUT TO:

The kitchen, where Jo and Steve listen to Henry the cook.

HENRY
Chén Syúng a, tsúng syǎu gèn
wǒ yīkwàr. Wǒmén lyǎ shr̃
túngsywé, yīkwàr shàng dàsywé,
shàng nèige hángkūng
gūngchéngsyī. Dzài dàsywéľi
aeronautics engineering....Nà,
tā dzài bànľi gùngkē tsài hǎu la.
Lǎu kǎ dīyī. Wǒ kǎu
dīszshŕwǔ; chywán bàn
szshŕlyòuge swyéshēng. Hāhāhā!
Lái Měigwó yǐhóu dzémma yàng?
Jǎubùdàu gūngdzwò, jǎubùdàu
gūngdzwò nǐ jŕdàu ba! Méirén
yàu, nǐ méiyǒu shémma bànfǎ.
Némma, jèisyē Měigwó rén yàu
shémma nē? Tā bùyàu rén gěi nǐ
gǎu shémma hángkūng
gūngchéng ma!....Tā jyòu shr̃
yàu nǐ dzwò shémma dǎnjywǎn,
egg roll, sweet sour pork, won ton
soup, jèisyē wànyǐr.

He reads an order and responds to Camera/Waiter.

Dzěmma? Five won ton soup yòu

lái le! Wǒ gèn nǐ jyǎng a, syàtsz̀
Lǎuměi yàu lái chī jèige, nǐ gèn
tā jyǎng: "We don't have won ton
soup, we have won ton spelled
backwards—'not now!'" Hāhāhā!

Some ingredients are stir-fried in a wok. Henry continues in VO.

Tāmāde! Nà hwěr gē hwéi chyù
le!...The funny thing was, the
other day he's bussing a table
and there came these friends of
his, colleagues of his from
Taiwan, lives in the United
States, in San Francisco. The
minute he saw those friends he
rushed from the back door and
never came back again...

CUT TO:

A table in the dining room, where people, speaking in Cantonese, are fighting over a check—with the only male at the
table managing to get it.

          HENRY (VO)
Jùnggwó rén ma, yàu myàndz
ma ...You know, the problem is, I
think this guy has too much pride,
too much pride.

     WOMAN AT TABLE
Haih, nīgo haih...

     SECOND WOMAN
Msái néih a. Dōu wah...

     THIRD WOMAN
Dím hóu yisi a. Sèhngyaht néih
chéng...

          MAN
Mgányiu la. Mgányiu.
Hahyātchi néihdeih.

FOURTH WOMAN
Hóu a. Hóu a.

FIFTH WOMAN
Dòjeh.

HENRY (VO)
Wǒ ľibàisż syōusyí, gèn nǐ dǎ
dyànhwà... Thursday, talk to you
later, okay?

JO (VO)
Okay.

HENRY (VO)
Bye bye, Jo.

8. EXT. CHINATOWN STREET—DAY

Jo and Steve walk down the street, involved in conversation.

STEVE
I tell you, $4,000 is a lot of money
for me, you know.

JO
Oh, you're going into that again.

STEVE
Yeah, sure. It's my money man,
yeah, I'm going into it.

JO
It's your money, I put some
money into it.

STEVE
Eh, you sure, you sure your
feelings about your ex-wife
doesn't have something to do
with the way you're treating this
Chan Hung thing?

JO
My ex-wife got nothing to do with

it. The divorce is over.

STEVE
I'm not talking about a divorce.
I'm talking about how you used
to feel about her, you know.
Being an FOB, and everything.

JO
I feel alright. I'm okay.

STEVE
Eh.

JO
Yeah?

STEVE
That Tuesday before Christmas—

JO
Yeah, yeah.

STEVE
You know what I'm talking about?

JO
Yeah, I remember.

STEVE
What?

JO
Something about what, the
mǐhnnaahp,*you talking about?

STEVE
Yeah, yeah, yeah. Chan Hung
comes in with that new, nice new
silver mǐhnnaahp,*right? So what,
you said something to him in
Chinese about you really liked
that right. So right there, man,
he takes the fucking jacket off
and he practically forces it on
you, you know.

*cotton padded jacket 棉袄

JO
What's wrong with that?

STEVE
No, no, no. So later on that day,
you know, you know, I said to
him, you know, I said, those are
real sharp pants, you going to
take them off for me too? And
fuck, he gets all embarrassed like
I was serious. He gets
embarrassed on me. Says (mimics
voice) "No, no, I not do that for
you." I says, "Chan Hung, I was
just kidding you, you know."
He says, "No, no, I never do that
for you," you know. That's, that's
all I'm trying to say, that's what
I mean, he reminds me of my ol'
man that way, you know.
Fucking embarrassing.

9. INT. JO'S APARTMENT—NIGHT

Jo sits at the table with a drink. He walks over to the bay window, peers out, and pulls down the shade.

JO (VO)
The FOBs, fresh off the boat, as
Steve calls them. Didn't come off
a boat—they came off of jumbo
jets. Steve doesn't realize that the
joke about the pants is really on
him. Chan Hung told me he
sometimes play up being an FOB
just to make Steve mad. Chan
Hung does have a sense of humor
that does not translate into
English. Like Don Rickles in
Chinese.

He switches on his code-a-phone.

STEVE (on tape)
Hey Jo, I found out that Chan
Hung spends a lot of time at that
Manilatown Senior Center. I'm

going to check it out. Why don't
you come with me.

10. INT. MANILATOWN SENIOR CITIZENS CENTER—DAY

SFX: Latin dance music, "Sabor A Mi"

Camera pans photographs on the walls which depict past
events and younger days. Pilipino men and women sit on
benches and chairs, enjoying the music. One couple gets up
and dances. A white-haired, bespectacled man stares blankly
ahead. Hand-held camera moves down the corridor to a back
office, where Jo and Steve question Presco, a young staff
worker.

> STEVE
> I'm looking for money, man.

> PRESCO
> You looking for money or you
> looking for Mr. Chan?

> JO
> Do you know where he is?

> PRESCO
> Well, we call him Hi Ho down
> here, right.

> JO
> Hi Ho?

> PRESCO
> Yeah.

> STEVE
> You know that old manong over
> there I was talking to?

> PRESCO
> Yeah. Reuben. Reuben. Yeah.

> STEVE
> He said he'd never seen anybody
> named Chan, but he comes down
> here every week.

PRESCO
Yeah, everybody down here calls
him Hi Ho.

JO
Why do they call him Hi Ho?

PRESCO
Hi Ho, because he always likes
Hi Ho cookies. He always has
them in his jacket.

Frankie, an oldtimer, enters the room.

Frankie!

FRANKIE
Are you looking for Mr. Chan?

JO
Yeah, yeah.

FRANKIE
I haven't seen him for the last
two weeks, and he was telling me
before that he might go back to
the old country.

PRESCO
No—how would we know where
to find him, though.

FRANKIE
Well, I tell you, he got his jacket
here.

Frankie removes a jacket from a wall hook.

PRESCO
That's not his jacket! Maybe it is.
Hey, there's crackers in here—it
is his jacket.

FRANKIE
Yes it is. This is his and he even

left his jacket here. He is still
intending to come back and go to
work here.

Frankie pulls some papers from the pocket.

JO
Hey, you got something there.
Let's take a look.

The group crowds around.

FRANKIE
Now here it is, here, here.

PRESCO
It's a will. Is it a will?

JO
Oh, this is in Chinese.

FRANKIE
Yeah, well, it doesn't matter if it's
writing in Chinese or Hindu, but
we got the stuff right here.

Group laughter.

JO
Let me take a look, let me take a
look. Maybe I can see what it is.

Jo unfolds a newspaper clipping. The headline reads "State's
Oldest Murder Defendent—Man Charged with Murder at Age
85"

PRESCO
Translate it, yeah. But I don't
think he would go back home. He
said that one thing he wanted to
do is go back home, but because
something, he couldn't get the
fare back, or who knows?

FRANKIE
You don't know the Oriental

people. When they say they
haven't got it, don't worry, they
got it. He has money. In China,
but not right now.

                STEVE
My $4,000 bucks, man, he got it.

                FRANKIE
Any time but right now.

                JO
Are you sure?

                FRANKIE
I cannot be so sure, but that is
my strong belief, that's he's back
there. Because three weeks ago
when I saw him, he was still
thinking about having property
parted between the three
brothers. He said, "If I can't do
this right now, maybe I'll be too
old to go back to China and
settle this settlement. Now I'm
gonna do it now while I'm
still happy and I have money to
go back to America." Because if
he doesn't go now, he will never
be going back anymore.

CUT TO:

Couples dancing to mariachi music in the main hall.

                PRESCO (VO)
Hi Ho, he like coming down
because he likes to listen to music
and he's crazy about all kind
different kinds of music. But his
favorite was mariachi and his
best friend down here was one of
the musicians. And so last week
this musician friend, he just got up,
and he couldn't play music any
more. He just got up. He just got up

> like that—he didn't say nothing to
> nobody.

CUT TO:

Presco continuing the conversation in the back office.

> If you see him walking down the
> street I'm sure you would cross
> the street because he'll drool on
> you. I mean, he has no control
> over his legs or how he walks,
> you know. You'd pass him off as
> drunk, right. You put him behind
> a piano and he'll make you cry
> because he was a musician and
> he was used to being in the
> spotlight, right, and one time he
> woke up, and he woke up that
> way. He was all—

                    JO
> You mean just like that?

                  PRESCO
> Yeah. We took him to all kinds of
> neurologists and they said they
> don't know, and so just hanging
> around with him and he said the
> only way he could find someone
> to help him, to make him well, is
> like, um, whenever you see him
> walking around, especially in the
> rain, he's looking at a puddle,
> right? He says he told me the
> only person who could fix him is
> that person in the puddle.

                    JO
> Oh, wow.

                  PRESCO
> Make sense?

                    JO
> Makes some kind of sense being

in a sense it's uh—

PRESCO
It's nonsense.

JO
It's the relationship.

STEVE
Boy, it makes a lot of sense to me,
man.

JO
Sure, there's a relationship. Don't
you think that—

PRESCO
You guys are looking for Mr.
Chan—why don't you look in the
puddle?

11. EXT. STREET—DAY

Steve and Jo lean against their cab, talking. Steve reads a
newspaper.

JO
I'm still trying to connect Chan
with that clipping, that clipping
we found in his pocket. This old
guy killed somebody over this
flag-waving incident.

12. EXT. TUNNEL—DAY

Jo drives his cab through a tunnel as a newscast blares over the
radio.

ANNOUNCER
In San Francisco police are
holding 87-year-old Sung Kim
Lee in the shooting death of
another elderly man in the
hallway of a Chinatown rooming
house. 79-year-old Chun Wang
was found outside his room just

before noon today after residents
reported the two men were
fighting. Officers say the two
men had been carrying on a
political feud since the Chinese
New Year's parade, a feud that
had forced neighbors to call in
the police several other times in
the last two weeks. Lee, a
supporter of the People's Republic
of China, was involved in a flag-
waving incident during the
parade that apparently angered
his anti-Communist pro-Taiwan
neighbor.

CUT TO:

News clippings and photographs of the Chinese New Year's
flag-waving incident.

JO (VO)
This year when the Chinese
community itself couldn't agree
on which Chinese flag to wave
during the New Year's parade,
the mayor told the community
that only the American flag
should be represented. The
organizers of the parade who
were all Taiwan supporters
ignored the mayor's
recommendation and waved the
Taiwan flag regardless. During
the parade when some PRC
supporters protested the waving
of the Taiwan flag, a fight took
place.

13. EXT. STREET—DAY

Steve and Jo talk at the side of their cab.

STEVE
The Chinese, they love to fight,
man. Just give them a reason,

man, over mahjong, over food,
anything, man. But that, shit,
Chinatown is still owned by
Taiwan. Just because America is
hip to New China, that don't
mean shit to these guys over
here.

JO (VO)
It's strange enough that an 87-
year-old man would kill someone
over what flag to wave for the
New Year's parade, but what I
really don't understand is why
Chan Hung had the article about
the murder in his coat pocket. I
decided to find out more about it.

14. INT. STEVE AND AMY'S KITCHEN—NIGHT

Jo sits at the table sharing his hunches about Chan with
Steve and Amy.

JO
Chan Hung—Chan Hung—Chan
Hung took some pictures. He's
got to have something to do with
it. Some guy at work said Chan
Hung took some pictures at the
Chinese New Year's parade, that
Taiwan supporters were beating
up the PRC guys.

AMY
That'd be great. That's gonna be
hot evidence.

STEVE
Wait, wait, you say Chan Hung
took pictures of these PRC guys?

AMY
That's great. And if that's so,
they could use those pictures to
hang each other.

                    STEVE
I wonder if Chan...that sounds
pretty heavy. Do you think he
split because of that?

                    JO
I went back to talk to the cook,
too, you know that cook?

                    AMY
Oh Henry, the one in the Golden
Dragon.

                    JO
Yeah.

                    AMY
That wonderful, beautiful form-
fitting Samurai Night Fever shirt
with that bod.

                    STEVE
Baggy, man, baggy and ugly.

                    STEVE
Hey, have you ever heard Henry
rap about China? How he
identifies with all those people?

                    JO
Yeah, rock me to the moon?

                    AMY
Oh yes. Help the poor and needy.

15. EXT. ROOFTOP—DAY (flashback)*

Henry the cook, dressed in a three-piece suit, converses with
Jo, partly in Mandarin.

SFX: Street traffic; passing Chinese drum and cymbal music

                    JO (VO)
Henry thought that Chan Hung
went back to China because it
was just too difficult for him to

*See pp. 86-87 for English translation and pp. 97-98 for Chinese character text for
this entire scene

identify with the mainland
Chinese from 8,000 miles away.
That makes Chan Hung out to be
too simple. He had a lot more on
his mind than that. Chan Hung
once told me that he wouldn't go
back to China until he had
achieved something in America.

HENRY
Dzài Měigwó nǐ yàu dzwò yīge
Jùnggwó rén na. Wéiyīde bànfǎ.
Nǐ yàu hé nine hundred...you ı—
...you have to identify with the
nine hundred million Chinese in
China...

JO
(interrupting)
Ah, wait a minute—

HENRY
...Then you have, you have
some, some meaning there.

JO
Wait a minute. But you know
here are, you know we're Chinese
here too. There are a lot of
Chinese. You're Chinese here too.

HENRY
You are...you know...dzài jèr,
dzài dzài dzài dzài Měigwó
rénjyā jyòu bá nǐ dàng wàigwó
rén kàn. You are foreigners here,
you know that. You don't belong
here. People consider you a
foreigner. You're, you're born
here, right? Nǐ...nǐ shēng—
A.B.C.?

JO
Right.

BOTH
(in unison)
A.B.C.

HENRY
You're A.B.C. Rénjyā bá nǐ
dàngwéi Měigwó rén ma? They
still consider you as a foreigner.

JO
Yeah, I know, but you know—
here, right here, we have to do
something. We have to fight.

HENRY
Fight, fight for what? Fight for
recognition? You know how long
we've been here? Wǒmén lái jèr
yībǎidò nyán la. Yībǎidò nyán,
ránhóu jyā wǔshŕwàn Jùnggwó
rén dzài jèr. Half million
Chinese, one hundred years. If
they don't recognize us, they
don't want to recognize us, and
they will not recognize us. You
know what I mean? Wǒmén jèi
yīběidz jyòu jŕ gwò yītsż.
Kělyàndehén na. Rénde yīběidz
gwǒ yītsż. Dzwò dyǎr yǒuyīyīde
shŕ. You...you only live once. So
we should do something
more...more significant. How's
that, eh?

16. INT. STEVE AND AMY'S APARTMENT—NIGHT

Amy, Steve, and Jo sit at the table, continuing their
conversation about Henry.

AMY
You know that guy is so filthy
rich, man.

JO
Really?

                    AMY
          Yeah, that's how he can afford to
          help the needy and the poor.

                    STEVE
          That's just a front, man.
          Whenever anyone comes in the
          restaurant. That guy might have
          a dirty smock, man, but he's got
          a face of jade. That guy is
          loaded—

                    AMY
          Face of jade?

                    STEVE
          —just like all those new guys
          coming in from Taiwan and Hong
          Kong with all that money. They're
          buying up all over the place. They
          don't care about—

                    AMY
          That's why he can afford to want
          to help. He has eight restaurants
          and three of them are within two
          blocks of Clement Street.

                    STEVE
          Couple of cat houses on
          Broadway...

17. EXT. STREET—DAY

A montage of Chinatown street scenes. Jo sits in his cab
watching Chan Hung's hotel. He and Steve walk down the
street.

SFX: "Where is My Home?" (a Chinese pop song about someone without a home, just wandering)

                    JO (VO)
          Chan Hung lived at Hotel St.
          Paul. Steve and I decided to take
          turns and watch the hotel.

18. INT. HOTEL ST. PAUL—DAY

Jo and Steve enter the hotel and climb a long flight of stairs
to Chan Hung's room. They knock on the door; there is no
response.

                         STEVE
            He ain't in.

                       NEIGHBOR
            (from behind closed door)
            Looking for Chan Hung? Look
            for the woman who took picture.

Jo and Steve move toward the neighbor's door.

                          JO
            Eh, we're friends of Chan
            Hung's. My name's Jo.

                       NEIGHBOR
            Hey Jo, get the facts, man. Dum-
            da-dum-dum. Look for the woman
            who took the photographs from
            Chan Hung's room.

                          JO
            What about the woman who took
            those pictures? Can you tell us
            more?

                       NEIGHBOR
            Hey Jo, you want Chan Hung's
            mail? They gave it all to me.
            Your woman don't want 'em
            either.

                          JO
            Eh, is she a relative? Can we
            come in and talk to you? Can we
            see the girl?

                       NEIGHBOR
            Eh Jo, you seen Rockford last
            night? Old rerun. Woman in red
            took photographs.

JO
What kind of pictures are they?
Can you let us in so we can look
at them?

NEIGHBOR
Hey, you Chinese, Jo?

STEVE
Are you Chinese?

NEIGHBOR
I Chinese. I don't like Chinese,
though.

JO
Hey, hey, what about that
woman. Is she a relative of Chan
Hung's?

NEIGHBOR
Hey Jo, are you police?

JO
No, no, no, no. We're not cops.

STEVE
No, business, business partners
of Chan Hung's.

NEIGHBOR
I don't want nothing to do with
Chinese.

JO
Hey—hello? Hey.

STEVE
Can we talk to you for a minute,
sir? We just need to talk to you.

JO
Hey, hello.

Steve raises clasped hands like a gun and backs against the wall in a "ready" position.

> STEVE
> Magnum would go—

Jo shakes his head and motions Steve to leave with him.

19. INT. CHAN HUNG'S ROOM—NIGHT

A neon sign outside reads "Hotel St. Paul." A widening shaft of light fills the floor as a door opens into a darkened room. Angle on a pair of legs walking slowly in. The room is explored.

> JO (VO)
> That night I went back to the hotel and persuaded the manager to let me into Chan Hung's room with the pass key. I didn't find anything except a bunch of paper. One, a newspaper with an article about the flag-waving incident. Two, another newspaper with an article ripped out. And three, something did seem to be missing from one of the walls. It might be the photograph of the flag-waving incident. Maybe Chan's neighbor was right. The facts, nothing but the facts. I checked the date of the cut-up newspaper I found in Chan Hung's room. It matched the date of the articles we found in Chan Hung's jacket about the old man who murdered his neighbor.

20. EXT. STREETS—DAY

Jo hits the streets in his cab.

> JO (VO)
> I went all over Chinatown to find out more about the murder. I tracked down the old man. He

was out on bail, but he refused to
talk to me. He told me to look for
the woman.

21. INT. JO'S APARTMENT—NIGHT

SFX: Watchdogs barking

Jo enters the room and turns off the tape recorder. The
barking ceases. He flips on the code-a-phone.

> STEVE (on tape)
> Hey, why aren't you ever home.
> I'm always talking to this god-
> damned machine. This morning
> a woman came to the garage,
> right, looking for Chan Hung
> and so I just hung out and
> waited for her to split so I
> followed her home. Maybe she's
> the woman everyone's been
> talking about. I thought I'd wait
> for you so we can go talk to her
> together, alright?

22. EXT. RESIDENTIAL STREET—DAY

Steve and Jo stand on the sidewalk outside an apartment
building. Mrs. Chan and Jenny (Chan Hung's wife and
daughter) cross the street. Jo steps forward and introduces
himself and Steve. Jo enters the building with Mrs. Chan and
Jenny while Steve waits outside.

23. INT. MRS. CHAN'S APARTMENT—DAY

Mrs. Chan, Jenny, and Jo enter the apartment. This and the
previous scene are shot from POV of Popo (grandmother), a
silent observer who watches the street scene from the window,
then sits down when the others enter the apartment.

> MRS. CHAN
> Come on in. I'm afraid I have
> another appointment. I really
> don't have a lot of time. Would
> you like some coffee?

                    JO
        Yes, please.

                MRS. CHAN
        Okay.

Jenny walks to the door of the television room.

                JENNY (to CAM)
        What are you watching, Popo?

Jenny turns to look at the television set. After a few seconds, she
shrugs, and exits. Jo and Mrs. Chan continue their conversation
in the adjoining room.

                    JO
            You speak very good English,
            Mrs. Chan.

                MRS. CHAN
            Oh, call me Liz. You see, my
            father used to work for the
            American Consulate in Taiwan
            and I went to American school
            there.

Their conversation is interrupted by a blast of Cantonese rock
music from a bedroom stereo.

            Excuse me.

Mrs. Chan exits, and shouts off-camera.

            Jenny, turn that down. Jenny, turn
            that down.

She returns to the room.

            He changed.

But the stereo volume has not. She walks toward the bedroom
again.

            Jenny, it's still too loud!

She approaches Jo again.

> I'm sorry. Here, why don't you
> take some oranges. Here, take
> one for your friend outside. I'm
> really sorry, but I have to get
> ready.

24. EXT. STREET—DAY

CU (close-up shot) of Steve's hands peeling an orange.

> JO (VO)
> Other than the tangerines, which
> is supposed to bring good luck, I
> didn't get very much out of Mrs.
> Chan. She didn't seem too
> concerned about her husband
> missing. She said that Chan
> Hung changed after he came to
> America.

CUT TO:

A head shot of Mrs. Chan.

> MRS. CHAN
> My husband changed after he
> come over. He doesn't like it here.
> He doesn't even want to apply for
> American citizen. He's too
> Chinese.

CUT TO:

Steve and Jo on the sidewalk next to their cab. Steve finishes
peeling the orange and starts eating.

> JO (VO)
> Apparently Chan Hung's been
> separated from her for over a
> year. But he never mentioned
> anything to me about having a
> family. Steve wanted to go to the
> police about Chan Hung. He
> didn't think I would get very far

with my investigation. I
persuaded Steve to wait a few
days.

Jo reads a newspaper article to Steve.

                    JO
All those Filipino teenagers
standing around. "Hey, they
better not fuck with this Flip."
Pulled back his trenchcoat and
pulls out a 22-calibre pistol. Here,
read.

He hands the newspaper to Steve.

                    STEVE
Oh yeah. The other side though,
you gotta read the other side, the
Chicano goes, "We know them
Flips are packing, but you take
away their pieces and they won't
be shit." He pulled out a 12″
switchblade, whoo! "Eh, I don't
need this filero* to kill those
Flips. I can handle those
motherfuckers with my bare
hands." Cops have no leads.
Man, what else is new?

A wide-eyed Jo leans toward his nephew.

What's wrong with you, boy? Get
out of my face.

                    JO
Is this the same guy who wants
to go to the cops about Chan
Hung?

                    STEVE
Yeah.

                    JO
Yeah?

*knife

STEVE
Hey, I ain't saying the cops are
cool—I didn't say that. All I'm
saying is that they're getting
paid by our tax money to do
something. That they should
follow up on the leads. They're
good at that kind of stuff. They
should do it for us. We shouldn't
have to worry about it.

JO
Two-faced schizophrenic
Chinaman, uh? Contradiction,
bicultural.

STEVE
Nah, nah. I'm not two-faced. Eh,
two of my ex-partners I used to
run with in high school, they're
cops man. Nah, it's a fine line
between a criminal and a cop.

JO
Uh huh.

STEVE
Forget you, man. You don't
understand.

25. INT. NEWCOMER'S LANGUAGE CENTER—DAY

Jo enters the Center. A white instructor leads his class in
English drills.

JO (VO)
Steve says he feels stupid
running around with me asking
about Chan Hung. So I went by
myself to see my friend George,
who runs the Newcomer's
Language Center.

INSTRUCTOR AND
STUDENTS (in unison)
Are you ready, are you ready, are

you ready to go?
Not quite, not quite, just a
minute, don't rush me.
Hurry up, hurry up, hurry up,
hurry up.
I'll be ready in a minute, in a
minute, in a minute.
I can't find my keys,
I can't find my keys!

CUT TO:

The Director's office, where Jo sits down to an appointment
with George, the Center's administrator.

> GEORGE
> Chan Hung, Chan Hung...

> JO
> Was he a student here?

> GEORGE
> I think he was, now of course we
> run through a lot of—

He looks through some papers at his desk.

> Chan Hung—Let me see, I think
> I seem to remember him.

He walks over to his files.

> Oh, there he is.

CUT TO:

George sitting at his desk.

> Well, Chan Hung is uh, has the
> typical problem like most of us
> one time or another have as
> immigrants. He came here and
> he wanted to be, continue to be
> Chinese, everything. Thinking,
> doing things and all that and of
> course that presents a problem.

Now, on the other extreme you got some people who come here and they immediately want to assimilate like the rest of the white Americans, and that also presents a problem. They're not white. And I think the way we need to deal with it is to be Chinese American—to take the good things from our background and also trying to take the good things from this country to enhance our lives.

CU of a box of Sun Wah Kue's apple pie.

                    GEORGE
Sun Wah Kue's apple pie. It is a definite American form, you know. Pie, okay, and it looks like any other apple pie, but it doesn't taste like any other apple pie when you eat it and that's because many Chinese baking techniques has gone into it and when we deal with our everyday lives that's what we have to do.

                    JO (VO)
George didn't know anything specific about Chan Hung. Got into a spiel about Chinatown politics again.

                    GEORGE
...missing the boat because we're not spending enough time to try to enhance the lives of Chinese here in America and I often joke with them because I talk to both sides all the time. Let me give you an instance. It's sort of funny. Like October 1st lot of people in the left wing want to have a parade in Chinatown and October 10 they always had a

parade in Chinatown, and that
parade sort of expend a lot of
energy and get a lot of manpower
to go into it so I have been
proposing to them for several
years now—they haven't bought
it yet but I think eventually they
might—I say, why have a parade
at October 1st and why have
another one October 10. Why can't
we combine the two and have it in
Oct. 5 and the left wing will take
the left hand side of the street,
the right wing will take the right
hand side of the street and you
go have your parade. Because
basically, other than the people
participating in the parade, the
people don't give a damn.

26. EXT. GRANT AVENUE—DAY

Jo walks down Grant Avenue with his jacket over his
shoulder.

JO (VO)
I was amused by George's talk on
Chinatown's politics. Even
though I had heard it many
times before. The punch line
George forgot this time was how
the politicians would walk down
the middle of the street and
shake hands with people on both
sides.

27. EXT. STREET—DAY

Jo pulls his cab to the curb and honks his horn. Steve
approaches the car. Jenny and a friend walk down the street
and Jenny recognizes them.

JENNY
Hey, you guys were at my house
the other day, right?

Steve recognizes her, and steps back from the car to greet them.

STEVE
(To Jo) That's Chan Hung's
daughter. (To Jenny and friend)
Yeah, this is Jo Jo and I'm
Steve Chan, Choy, Chan, Choy.

He reaches out to shake hands. They respond with soul shakes. He smiles and shifts to his best jive talk.

Hey, what's hap'ning, what's
hap'ning with you, too? How are
you today? Alright.

JENNY'S FRIEND
Hey, this dude doesn't even know
his name.

STEVE
Hey, what's new with you? That's
Mr. Charlie Chan and I'm his
number one son, The Fly
(laughs). You know, you know it's
like, I was trying to talk to your
father one day you know, we was
tripping in the cab. That Mrs.
Chong over at, down at these
mahjong tables, she just don't
know how to run that mahjong
table, man. She got to get them
four inches of foam you know, get
them four inches of foam, so when
the mahjong hits, man, it tell the
truth. You got to tell the truth. You
got to get them people's money. Got
to get them old ladies' money. Come
down there, get that money. Got to
tell the truth. You know what I
mean? You guys don't know what's
happening—

JENNY
Hey, who do you think you are
anyway? You think you're

Richard Pryor or something like
that?

STEVE
Hey, no, I ain't Richard Pryor,
man, you know, Richard Pryor—
anyway, so your dad, like, we're
not into no trouble. We just want
to know where he is, you know.

JENNY
Well what kind of jive did my
mom tell you about my dad
anyway?

STEVE
I wasn't talking to her you know.
I guess she's cool. She gave us
some oranges from Taiwan.

JENNY
Well you know, the only reason I
ask is cause, uh, well you could
see they're not too much the
same. When we came over here,
she like, adjusted. Well you know
she's been hassling with it a lot
too, but she gets on my dad's case
because he's not successful like
Mr. Lee.

JO
Who is Mr. Lee?

JENNY
He's our sponsor. He's got an
office, you know, in Chinatown
above Imperial Palace. He might
be the one you want to talk to. I
think my dad went to see him
about something last week.

STEVE
Well, maybe we'll go down to Mr.
Lee's tomorrow. So thanks a lot
for telling us about it. If you see

your dad let him know that we're looking for him, alright? And we don't mean him no harm. You guys want some, I got some spare change, go get yourself an ice cream cone, man?

                    JENNY
Who do you think we are, kids?

                    STEVE
Well, you don't look like my grandpa. (laughs) This is bullshit, man. Catch you later.

                 JENNY'S FRIEND
Keep the change.

28. INT. LEE'S OFFICE—DAY

Jo enters the office and approaches the receptionist's desk.

SFX: Ticking clock

                    JO
I have an appointment with Mr. Lee.

                  SECRETARY
Mr. Lee is on the phone right now. Please take a seat.

                    JO
Thank you.

Jo sits down and scans the room. He sees a clock which reads 4:50, traditional Chinese wall altars with statues of deities and red paper proverbs, and some professional awards and diplomas. He sees a second clock which reads 3:00. Lee enters the room.

                    LEE
Oh, how're you doing?

                    JO
Hi, I'm Jo.

LEE
Jo? Come on in.

The two enter Lee's office and sit down.

JO
You know what we talked about—

LEE
Yeah, right. Did you want to see
your friend, somehow?

JO
Well, you know I'm looking for
him and uh, we have some
business deals that we, and I
haven't been able to find him for
the past week or so.

LEE
Week or so. Yeah. The last time I
saw him was over a week ago. He
had an accident we were
handling. He reported it. (Phone
rings) Excuse me. Hello. Oh yeah,
Harry? Yes, Harry, oh yeah, I
sent him up there, Harry. Did he
give you a bad time? Oh, he did?
He's one of these wise guys you
know, these Chinese fellows. You
have to be a little smarter, Harry.
Tell you what. How much is the
job? $380? I tell you what to do.
Tell him it's about $600 okay?
Why? This is it, ya dum dum, you
know how Chinese are. You still
dealing with these customers, by
the time he get out your door he
only going to pay you about $300,
you nut. Oh, oh, you caught the
idea, eh, about time. No wonder.
You don't do that, you be out of
business. Yeah. Yeah. You pay for
the mechanic and all that. Yeah.
He gotta pretty bad smash. Right
in the rear end. So he be up there

to see you very soon. Yeah. Don't
listen to the wife neither, will
you? Your wife gonna give it to
you. Okay. You know what to do
now, huh? Okay, alright, alright.
I'll see you later.

JO

I guess you don't know where Mr.
Chan is?

LEE

I haven't seen him for the past
week or so. I've got to find him.
He has to report to me. I kind of
sponsored him here. I have a
hard time explaining to him. I
always generally, when they buy
insurance, I always draw them a
diagram of an intersection.
Sometimes they, hard to educate
them. There's one, there was a
colored guy. He stopped at the
stop sign there at Pine Street, it's
one way. He's going home and I
don't know how—he didn't hit the
brakes fast enough—he just
tapped the colored guy, and the
colored guy said, well I'm going
to call the police, and I told him
before, I said anytime you hit
somebody in the rear, give him
your name, your license number,
and then tell him my agent will
take care of it. And he says,
"Yeah, I did all that. But he tell
me to wait." I said, "What the
hell's the matter with you—he got
a gun on you?" He said no.
"Then what the hell you waiting
for?" He said, "You know, these
big black guys, I'm afraid they'll
hit me." I said, "He can't hit
you."

JO (VO)
Chan Hung wasn't just another
dumb Chinaman like the guy in
Mr. Lee's story. Maybe Mr. Lee
and Mrs. Chan don't know the
whole story. Chan Hung was the
brains behind his brother's
invention of the first word
processing system in Chinese.

29. EXT. CHINATOWN—DAY

A montage of Chinatown scenes. Aerial views of the
community. The photograph of the flag-waving incident. A
newspaper clipping reporting the occurrence. Jo sits in his cab
thinking.

JO (VO)
Today a community newspaper
published a photograph of the
flag-waving incident. But some
people claim that it was of
another flag-waving incident two
years ago. People think it was
published to take the heat off of
finding the real one. This is all
too confusing.

30. INT. JO'S APARTMENT—NIGHT

Jo rummages through his apartment kitchen.

JO (VO)
I went home to get a bite to eat.
There was only a piece of leftover
pizza. Chan Hung used to always
talk about how Marco Polo stole
everything from us, first pasta,
then pizza. Too bad the Chinese
didn't have tomatoes. But I
shouldn't complain. The only
thing I use my oven for is to store
gadgets. I guess I'm no gourmet
Chinese cook and I'm no Charlie
Chan either, although I did start
watching some of his reruns for

cheap laughs. Charlie says,
"When superior man have no
clue, be patient, maybe he become
lucky."

31. EXT. CHAN HUNG'S CAB—NIGHT

Jo searches Chan's cab and uncovers two more clues.

> JO
> The next night I was cleaning out
> the cab that Chan Hung was
> driving the day he disappeared. I
> found a letter in Chinese and a
> gun under the front seat.

32. INT. MONTAGE—NIGHT

SFX: Suspenseful music

Quick cuts of Jo at home, Chan's dark apartment, the
flag-waving incident photograph, a letter in Chinese, CU of
the Chinese characters in the letter.

> JO (VO)
> The police are still looking for the
> gun the old man used to shoot his
> neighbor. Steve thinks it's the
> gun I found in Chan Hung's cab.
> He thinks that Chan Hung was
> the one who actually killed the
> neighbor and that the old man
> was just covering up for him. I
> tried to contact the old man
> again. He still refuses to see me.
> But he told me that Chan Hung
> had nothing to do with the
> murder or the flag-waving
> incident. He said that Chan
> Hung just got paranoid and made
> everything up in his own mind. I
> took the letter to George to have
> him translate it. The letter was
> from Chan Hung's brother. The
> brother told Chan Hung that it
> was quite possible that the people

from the left were after him also.
He told Chan Hung that with
people in politics it was better to
be careful. He didn't think Chan
Hung was being too paranoid.

33. INT. GEORGE'S OFFICE—DAY

George examines Chan's letter for Jo.

> GEORGE
> Now let me ask you about this
> letter here. Where did he live
> when he disappeared?

> JO
> Well, he was living in some hotel
> in Chinatown.

> GEORGE
> That would be this address. See.
> The letter was actually sent to
> another address. Now maybe you
> have to check out that former
> address. Now that's what we call
> in the detective trade a good clue.
> Of course you don't look like
> anybody's conception of a Charlie
> Chan.

They both laugh.

> JO
> Not me. You do, George. Hey, I
> see somebody's waiting for you
> outside. Thanks a lot, George.

> GEORGE
> Well if you need any help why
> don't you come back and talk to
> me on it.

> JO
> Sure, thanks George.

GEORGE
Okay. See you, Jo.

34. EXT. RESIDENTIAL STREET—DAY

Jo converses on the street with a young man, who points
to an upstairs apartment.

JO (VO)
I went to the other address.
Nobody was there. A young man
who lived in the building told me
that Chan Hung used to live
there with his family but he
moved six months ago with the
other woman.

35. EXT. JO'S CAB—DAY

Jo sits in his parked cab, observing various women in
Chinatown.

36. INT. JO'S APARTMENT—EVENING

SFX: The phone rings.

Jo lifts the receiver.

WOMAN'S VOICE
Stop asking questions about
Chan Hung.

JO
Eh, who is this?

SFX: Dead signal

37. EXT. STREETS—DAY

Jo drives his cab through the streets. Driver's POV. Shots
dissolve into each other with the passing time.

JO (VO)
So, the other woman finally
appears. Now I'm really confused.
Maybe she took the real picture of

the flag-waving incident and had
the wrong one published, maybe
to cover for Chan Hung. Maybe
Chan Hung really did kill that
guy instead of the old man.
Maybe if I know this and
somebody knows that I know,
maybe they don't want me to
know.

38. EXT. STREETS—DAY

Jo walks down the street, periodically glancing behind him. Is
he being followed? He drives in his cab, anxiously checking
his rear view mirror. He makes a phone call, and buys a
newspaper, all the while looking about him.

SFX: Chase music, building in excitement

39. INT. CAFE—DAY

Jo sits alone at a table with a drink.

>   JO (VO)
> It's easy to see how someone can
> get paranoid. I feel like I'm in the
> same mess Chan Hung was in,
> except I'm not even sure what the
> mess is or how much of it is in
> my own mind.

40. EXT. PIER—DAY

In the distance, two people row a boat slowly across the water.
Fishermen lean over the wharf wall with their poles.

>   JO (VO)
> Hate to tell Steve that our last
> lead got us nowhere. He's really
> getting worried about the money.
> He's been pressing me about
> going to the cops. I don't think
> the cops can do anything about
> finding Chan Hung. There's
> probably more than three Chans
> on the missing persons list on

62

any given day. Besides, the only
picture I have of Chan Hung
won't give them that much to
work with.

Jo meets Steve. They walk down the pier, hands in pockets,
and air their growing differences.

JO
You know, it's hard enough for
guys like us who's been here so
long to find an identity, I can
imagine Chan Hung, somebody
from China coming over here and
trying to find himself.

STEVE
Aw, that's a bunch of bullshit
man. That identity shit, man,
that's old news, man. It happened
ten years ago.

JO
It's still going on.

STEVE
Bullshit. That don't mean
nothing. I ran into an old friend
of mine downtown, I pick him up,
you know, driving. We used to run
together in high school, right.
Him and me, the same, and the
rest of my buddies. He was all
decked out in his GQ fucking look
you know, with his fucking
Lóuhfàan* girl friend, you know.
And he didn't want to talk to me,
man. He knew who I was and he
didn't want to talk to me. That's
because he's playing the game,
man. Fuck the identity shit. He
knew what he was doing. I knew
what I was doing. I could have
kicked his fucking ass. Eh. Ain't
nothing to it anymore. The
Chinese are all over this fucking

*Old foreigner (i.e., white) 老番

city, man. What do you mean
about identity? They got their
own identity. I got my identity.

JO
Look, a guy who's had, who had
it all in another area, in China,
he was almost upper class, and
he comes over here and he can't
find a job—how do you think it
feels?

STEVE
That's tough shit, man. Eh, fuck,
when I was in fucking 'Nam,
man, and I was getting shot at
by my own people—eh, the
Chinese are all over the city, why
are you tripping so heavy on this
one dude for, man?

JO
Because he's a friend.

STEVE
Eh, is he really a friend?

JO (VO)
He's a friend. You know, he gets
involved in this stupid accident of
his, huh, and the cop picks him
up, now he's involved in another
damn thing. I feel for him.

STEVE
(shouting)
It's just an accident man, just a
fucking car accident.

JO
It's not a car accident.

STEVE
What are you tripping on this
shit for? Hey, what's in this for
you man—why are you tripping

so heavy man? The guy is fucked,
he fucked up man, he fucked up,
he couldn't cope with it, he
couldn't cope with it.

JO
I feel for the guy because I can
understand him—alright? Maybe
you can't, but I can.

STEVE
Hey, I understand the situation
man. Don't tell me I don't
understand the situation. I just
want to know why you're tripping
so heavy on it for. Because
obviously to me man, the facts
are the guy is a fucking liar. He's
been lying to us. Everytime we go
to somebody different we hear a
different story. Here's how I see
it. If you're sick, you go see a
doctor right? If you're going nuts
you go see a shrink. If you need
some money, man, you go to a
bank or a loan company. You
know, somebody rips off your
money, if you don't have no
friends who can take care of it
you go to the cops and let them
take care of it.

JO
No. We don't go to the cops.

STEVE
Why the fuck don't we not go to
the cops?

JO
Because it's none of their damn
business, that's why.

STEVE
Bullshit! It's my fucking money
too, man. Now let's quit fucking
around with this bullshit.

                    JO
Look—

                  STEVE
Eh, we're no closer than when we
first started, man. In fact, we're
—I'm more confused, now I don't
even know the guy we're talking
about.

                    JO
Look, he didn't take that money.

                  STEVE
              (Interjects)
Then where's the money?

                    JO
We'll get it back. You so hot
about that money I'll give it to
you. I'll give you my money.

The two walk off in different directions and stand apart on the
pier.

41. INT. CAFE—DAY

Steve and Jo sit at a table with beers. They stare blankly in
front of them. Steve looks over at Jo. Neither says a word.

42. INT. RESTAURANT—DAY

Jo and Steve enter the restaurant, remove their baseball caps,
and approach the woman behind the bar.

                    JO
        Uh, is Jenny here?

                      BARTENDER
        Jenny?

                      STEVE
        Jenny. Jenny Chan?

The bartender looks puzzled.

                    BARTENDER
    No.

                    STEVE
                    (to Jo)
    I thought you said you talked to
    her.

                    JO
    I did. We called her on—

                    STEVE
    We got a phone call from here to
    meet her.

                    BARTENDER
    No, we have a private party phone.

                    STEVE
                    (to Jo)
    Do you speak Japanese? You
    were overseas weren't you?

Jenny walks into the room.

                    JENNY
    Hey you guys.

                    STEVE
    Hey Jenny.

                    BARTENDER
    Oh, her name is Shao Lui, not
    Jenny.

                    STEVE
    What? Shao, Shao Lui? Shao
    Lui?

                    JENNY
    Yeah, that's my Chinese name.

They move to a table near a window.

                    STEVE
    Want to sit here? So what's

happening with you? How's
school? Y'wanna smoke a joint?

                    JENNY
Let's go outside.

                    STEVE
So what's up?

                    JENNY
Nothing. What about you?

                    STEVE
Well, you said that you wanted to
talk to us.

                    JENNY
Oh. Just wanted to say hi.

                    STEVE
                 (laughing)
          She said—

Jenny hands Steve an envelope.

                    JENNY
Here's the money honey.

                    STEVE
You ain't bullshitting, are you.

                    JENNY
Told you he wouldn't bum you
out on a deal. It's all there.

Steve opens the envelope and finds a thick wad of $100 bills.

                    STEVE
God damn.

                    JO (VO)
Jenny didn't know where her
father was. She said that her
father apologized for not being
able to complete the cab deal. If
this were a TV mystery, an

68

important clue would pop up at
this time and clarify everything.

43. EXT. PORTSMOUTH SQUARE—DAY*

Jo walks up to Mr. Fong, a scholarly-looking man dressed in a
suit. They stand and talk in Cantonese at the edge of the park.

FONG
...m̀gin hóu noih. Néih hóu ma?

JO
Hóu... hóu... néih heui bīndouh
a?

FONG
Ngóh ngāamngāam hái
Jùnggwok Màhnfa Jūngsām
heui yíngóng fàanlàih a màh.

JO
Oh, yíngóng, góng mātyéh a?

FONG
Góng Jùnggwok màhnfa hái
Sàamfàahnsihge faatjín.

JO
Oh... roots, eh? Chinese roots.

FONG
Haih, haih, haih. Yātbùn yàhn
nē, yíwàih Jùnggwok màhnfa
nē, jauhhaih yātgo hóu
gáandàange. Jéuidò haih sihk a.
Eat Chinese food a gám lo.
Kèihsaht m̀haih gam
gáandàange. Jùnggwok màhnfa nē,
haih hóu fùngfu dòchói ge. Nàahm
bāk dōu yáuhdākfànbihtge.
Gú gàm jauh gánggà m̀tùhng la.
Haih ma? Peiyùh hóuchíh
màhnhohkséuhng
bíuyihnchēutlàih jauh
m̀yātyeuhng. Bākfòngge, néih

*See pp. 88-89 for English translation and pp. 99-100 for Chinese character text for
this entire scene

táiháh: "Tin chongchong, yéh
mohngmohng. Fùng chèui chóu
dài gin ngàuh yèuhng." Nīgo
haih bākgwokge fùnggwòng.
Hái nàahmfòng jauh m̀tùhng go
lo wóh. "Fùng chèui hùhng lòh
liht. Jyún sàn jauh lòhng póuh."
Nīdī haih nàahmfòngge
chïhngdiuh. Hái heikehk
séuhngbihn yātyeuhng haih
m̀tùhng. Kéuih bākfòng gódī nē:
"Yī mǎ lí lyǎu, Syī Lyáng jyè."
Bākgwokge chïhngdiuh. Hái
nàahmfòng nē, Yuhtkehk
léuihtáuh nē, yauh m̀tùhng lo
wóh. Néih tái: "Jihk yeuhng che
jiu, leih yàhn heui." Gám, nīdī
hóu kèihngaihge.

JO
Ah, you're a very good scholar,
Mr. Fong.

FONG
Oh, sáimāt gam haakhei la.
Waih, néih nīpáai dōu hóuchíh
yáuhdī sàmsih gam. Yáuh
mātyéh sih a?

JO
Ngóh séung wán go pàhngyáuh
a. (VO) Mr. Fong didn't come up
with the important clue, but he
did tell me that to solve the
mystery I had to think
Chinese...

FONG
...lohkháhlàih kïngháhgài
lā...yám bùi chàh lā...

JO (VO)
...He told me the Chinese lantern
riddle.

44. EXT. CAB—DAY

Steve and Jo relax in their cab, which is parked under the
Golden Gate Bridge. Steve reads a newspaper while Jo tells
him a story.

> JO
> There's this farmer right, he has
> a nice, beautiful farm, but one
> year there's a big drought. So
> he's got no money and the
> landlord says, look, I don't give a
> shit whether you've got money or
> not money. You're gonna have to
> pay me.

Steve peers out the window.

> STEVE
> We should have gone fishing
> today.

> JO
> Yeah. (humors Steve and
> continues his story) "You're
> gonna have to pay me." So the
> farmer says, "I got no money."
> The landlord says, "Look, money
> or no, you're gonna have to pay
> me, even if you have to send your
> daughter up to me." The farmer
> says, so, "Okay with me if she
> wants to go." Well the daughter
> doesn't want to go so she goes up
> to the guy and says, "Look, I
> don't want to come here and you
> know that." So the landlord says,
> "I'm a good guy, see, I'm a good
> guy. I'll give you a chance. You
> see those two doors over there?
> One leads outside, one leads right
> into my bedroom."

They both laugh.

JO

"—you make a decision." Well, he
knows damn well that both of
those doors are going to lead
right into his bedroom, right, and
the girl knows that too. (laughs)
The girl knows that too. So what
do you think—

STEVE

She wants it, man, she wants it
bad.

JO

(humoring him) Yeah, she wants
it bad. What do you think, what
do you think she says? You know
what that girl did? She was
smart. Strictly Chinese. She said,
"That door over there is not the
door that leads outside." Got it?
Huh? You got it?

STEVE

Got it.

JO
(Skeptically)
You got it. You got it.

STEVE

Got it.

JO

You got it.

STEVE

Yeah.

JO

Alright. You street-wise Chinese
eh, you didn't get anything. You
know what she was trying to do.
She was trying to use the
negative to emphasize the
positive. That is what she was
trying to do—now you get it?

They laugh.

> STEVE
>
> Who told you that one? Is that what these Chinese, is that what these Chinese scholars do when they're soaking in the hot tub with their Lóuhfàan* girlfriends, thinking up all this bullshit?

> JO
>
> With the feather, right?

> STEVE
>
> Eh, that stuff's too deep for me.

> JO
>
> You got it, eh? Pick a race, any race. Six race.

> STEVE
>
> I said, Family Jewels and Mindy's Surprise.

> JO
>
> Family jewels? You wanna hear another story?

> STEVE
>
> No, no.

> JO
>
> I got another story. Family jewels—

> STEVE
>
> Forget it.

CUT TO:

Rippling waves in a sunlit ocean.

45. INT. JO'S APARTMENT—DAY

Jo sits at the table with a drink, deep in thought.

---

*Old foreigner (i.e., white) 老番

> JO (VO)
> This mystery is appropriately
> Chinese. What's not there seems
> to have just as much meaning as
> what is there. The murder article
> is not there. The photograph's not
> there. The other woman's not
> there. Chan Hung's not there.
> Nothing is what it seems to be. I
> guess I'm not Chinese enough. I
> can't accept a mystery without a
> solution.

> PRESCO (VO)
> You think I said listen, but you
> don't listen. You guys got to look
> in the puddle.

CUT TO:

Jo sitting at a cafe table, in thought.

> PRESCO (VO)
> I mean, knowledge—it make us
> free, right? I been down here in
> Manilatown too long and I see, I
> see the regular things and
> everyday things and for years
> people do normal things, right,
> and then all of a sudden
> something happens, right? This
> guy disappears without a trace,
> without a reason. Nothing.

46. EXT. MONTAGE—DAY

Street scenes of Chinatown. People wait at the bus stop.
Others walk past, toting their shopping bags. A bus sporting a
"Gordon's Gin—It's Crystal Clear" poster drives past. Hold on
a shot of the ocean.

> JO (VO)
> I've already given up on finding
> out what happened to Chan
> Hung. But what bothers me is
> that I no longer know who Chan

Hung really is. Mr. Lee says
Chan Hung and immigrants like
him need to be taught everything
as if they were children. Mr. Fong
thinks that anyone who can
invent a word processing system
in Chinese must be a genius.
Steve thinks that Chan Hung is
slow with it, but sly when it
comes to money. Jenny thinks
that her father is honest and
trustworthy. Mrs. Chan thinks
her husband is a failure because
he isn't rich. Amy thinks he's a
hard-headed political activist.
The old man thinks that Chan
Hung is just a paranoid person.
Henry thinks that Chan Hung is
patriotic and has gone back to
the mainland to serve the people.
Frankie thinks Chan Hung
worries a lot about money and
his inheritance. He thinks Chan
Hung's back in Taiwan fighting
with his brother over the
partition of some property.
George thinks Chan Hung's too
Chinese and unwilling to change.
Presco thinks he's an eccentric
who likes mariachi music.

CUT TO:

Jo driving his cab.

The problem with me is that I
believe what I see and hear. If I
did that with Chan Hung I'll
know nothing because everything
is so contradictory. Here's a
picture of Chan Hung but I still
can't see him.

CUT TO:

A photo of Jo and Chan, the former standing in the sunlight,
the latter in the shadows.

47. EXT. CHINATOWN—DAY

A montage of sidewalk scenes, Chinese architecture, time-worn buildings, turtles swimming in pans, gung fu posters and giant fortune cookies in store windows. An elderly Chinese woman walks along her balcony, then grasps the railing and rocks back and forth, seemingly in time with the uptempo soundtrack. Montage continues with an Italian Market, skyscrapers of the neighboring financial district, dim sum restaurant displays, more elderly women on the street, and tinseled window dressing.

SFX: "Grant Avenue" sung by Pat Suzuki

END

Jo (Wood Moy) and Steve (Marc Hayashi) in conversation outside Chester's cafe.

Henry the cook (Peter Wang) sings "Fry Me to the Moon."

Jo (Wood Moy) wonders if someone is following him.

Steve (Marc Hayashi) and Jo (Wood Moy) following an argument over the missing Chan Hung.

photos by Nancy Wong

English Translation
of Scenes in Spoken Chinese

English Translation of Scene 7, pp. 20-26

7. INT. GOLDEN DRAGON RESTAURANT KITCHEN—DAY

SFX: Henry the cook singing "Fry Me to the Moon"

Dressed in a Samurai Night Fever t-shirt, Henry, speaking primarily in Mandarin, is busily reading orders, mixing sauces, wok-frying, and guzzling milk.

> JO (VO)
> Steve's joke reminded me of someone Chan Hung talks about a lot. The cook at the Golden Dragon who wears a Samurai Night Fever t-shirt, drinks milk, chain smokes, and sings "Fry Me to the Moon," all while he's cooking up five orders of sweet and sour pork.

> HENRY
> *...what's happening?*

He picks up an order on a slip of paper.

> *Ha! Three orders of sweet and sour pork! His mother's! These stinky old Americans from day to night just eat this. I really can't understand it. How can this stuff be so good to eat? Sweet and sour pork...His mother's! This sourness in my stomach...has come again!*

He drinks some milk.

> *Oh, his mother's!*

He takes another gulp.

> *This kitchen isn't fit for humans
> to work in. Let me tell you, your
> barber goes in circles around a
> chair for money. And so what
> about us overseas students?
> Overseas students fool around a
> stove with a wok spatula for
> money! Haha! His mother's!*

CUT TO:

The dining room of the restaurant. Camera POV (point-of-view) is that of a waiter taking orders from patrons. At one table, an older Chinese couple and their daughter discuss their choices, partly in Cantonese.

> DAUGHTER
> What about, what about a—*white
> cabbage?*

> FATHER
> *White cabbage's no good. How
> about stir-fried Chinese broccoli,
> okay?*

> MOTHER
> *Very tough...*

> DAUGHTER
> No, I want something with beef
> in it. (to CAM: camera) You have
> something with beef in it?

> MOTHER
> *Very fat...*

> DAUGHTER
> What about...

> FATHER
> *Why not roast duck, okay?*

>MOTHER
>*Roast duck's fat... let's eat*
>*chicken.*

>DAUGHTER
>No, that's too heavy, that's too
>heavy for lunch, mom... what
>about fish?

>FATHER
>(tentatively)
>*Steamed... steamed...*

>DAUGHTER
>Yeah, yeah... fish.

>FATHER
>*... rock cod.*

>DAUGHTER
>Yeah.

>MOTHER
>*Oh, okay.*

>DAUGHTER
>Yeah, that rock cod sounds good.

CUT TO:

Another table, where a young man hands back a dish of food
to the waiter.

>YOUNG MAN (to CAM)
>We didn't order this.

The young man shakes his head and turns to the young
woman next to him.

>YOUNG WOMAN
>... you know, did you see that
>movie...

Jo and Steve enter through the front door of the restaurant
and speak to a waitress.

                    WAITRESS
        He's working downstairs in the
        kitchen. You want to see him?

                    JO
        Yeah... *thanks.*

                    WAITRESS
        Okay, you go here (pointing) and
        go down.

                    JO
        Thanks... thanks...

Jo and Steve make their way through the dining room
towards the kitchen. We hear snatches of conversation
between the young man and woman.

                YOUNG WOMAN
        ... long time...

                YOUNG MAN
        ... long time ago...

                YOUNG WOMAN
        ... that's a good one... but
        another thing is a...

CUT TO:

Another table, occupied by a white man, a white woman, and
across the table two Chinese women, speaking partly in Cantonese, who cannot be seen directly but only via a reflection
in the mirror.

                CHINESE WOMAN
        ... really troublesome... don't
        say anymore... (referring to the
        white man) *a leaking gas demon*,*
        you really are! (giggles)

                WHITE WOMAN
        (to white man) What's lauhhei?
        (turns to the Chinese woman)
        What's lauhhei?

*idiom meaning "slow poke"

WHITE MAN
(starts to explain)
Lauhhei...

SECOND CHINESE WOMAN
(squeals)
Leaking gas!

WHITE WOMAN
Leaking what?

WHITE MAN
Lauhhei means... (others are all
laughing)... not together, not
together; I didn't do it.

CUT TO:

The kitchen, where Jo and Steve listen to Henry the cook.

HENRY
*Chan Hung, we've been together
since we were little. The two of us
were classmates, and went to the
university together to study
aeronautic engineering. At the
university...* aeronautics
engineering... *Now, he was good
in his classwork. Always passed
number one. I ended up
number forty-five; the whole class
had forty-six students. Hahaha!
After coming to America, what
happened? He couldn't find a job,
couldn't find a job—you know
about that. When no one wants
you, you don't have any way out.
So, what do these Americans
want? He doesn't want people to
let you do any work in aeronautic
engineering... He just needs you
to make all those egg rolls,* egg
roll, sweet sour pork, won ton
soup, *these little tricks.*

He reads an order and responds to Camera/Waiter.

How come? Five won ton soup
*once again! Let me tell you, next
time the Old American wants to
come here to eat this stuff, you
say to him:* "We don't have won
ton soup, we have won ton
spelled backwards—'not now!'"
Hahaha!

Some ingredients are stir-fried in a wok. Henry continues in
VO.

*His mother's! Now that will put it
to him!*... The funny thing
was, the other day he's bussing
a table and there came these
friends of his, colleagues of his
from Taiwan, lives in the United
States, in San Francisco. The
minute he saw those friends he
rushed from the back door and
never came back again...

CUT TO:

A table in the dining room, where people, speaking in Cantonese, are fighting over a check—with the only male at the
table managing to get it.

HENRY (VO)
Chinese need face... You know, the
problem is, I think this guy has
too much pride, too much pride.

WOMAN AT TABLE
Yes, this is...

SECOND WOMAN
*It's not necessary for you. I
already said...*

THIRD WOMAN
*How can we have any face? You
treat us everytime...*

MAN
*It's not important. It's not
important. Your turn next time.*

FOURTH WOMAN
Alright. Alright.

FIFTH WOMAN
Thank you...

HENRY (VO)
I have my day off on Thursday,
I'll give you a call... Thursday,
talk to you later, okay?

JO (VO)
Okay.

HENRY (VO)
Bye bye, Jo.

15. EXT. ROOFTOP—DAY (flashback)

Henry the cook, dressed in a three-piece suit, converses with Jo,
partly in Mandarin.

SFX: Street traffic; passing Chinese drum and cymbal music.

JO (VO)
Henry thought that Chan Hung
went back to China because it
was just too difficult for him to
identify with the mainland
Chinese from 8,000 miles away.
That makes Chan Hung out to be
too simple. He had a lot more on
his mind than that. Chan Hung
once told me that he wouldn't go
back to China until he had
achieved something in America.

HENRY
In America you have to be a
Chinese. That's the only way.
You have to nine hundred... you
i—... you have to identify with
the nine hundred million Chinese
in China...

JO
(interrupting)
Ah, wait a minute—

HENRY
... Then you have, you have
some, some meaning there.

JO
Wait a minute. But you know
here are, you know we're Chinese
here too. There are a lot of
Chinese. You're Chinese here too.

HENRY
You are... you know... *here, in in*

in in America people just look at
you as a foreigner. You are
foreigners here, you know that.
You don't belong here. People
consider you a foreigner. You're,
you're born here, right? *You... you*
*were born—*A.B.C.?

JO

Right.

BOTH
(in unison)

A.B.C.

HENRY

You're A.B.C. *Do people consider*
you as an American? They still
consider you as a foreigner.

JO

Yeah, I know, but you know—
here, right here, we have to do
something. We have to fight.

HENRY

Fight, fight for what? Fight for
recognition. You know how long
we've been here? *We came here*
over one hundred years ago. Over
one hundred years, and then
we've increased to five hundred
thousand Chinese here. Half
million Chinese, one hundred
years. If they don't recognize us,
they don't want to recognize us,
and they will not recognize us.
You know what I mean? *We will*
only live this life once. That's a
great pity. One lives one life, and
should do something more
significant. You... you only live
once. So we should do something
more... more significant. How's
that, eh?

English Translation of Scene 43, pp. 68-69

43. EXT. PORTSMOUTH SQUARE—DAY

Jo walks up to Mr. Fong, a scholarly-looking man dressed in a suit. They stand and talk in Cantonese at the edge of the park.

FONG
*...haven't seen you in a long
time. How are you?*

JO
*Okay...okay...where are you
going?*

FONG
*I've just come from giving a talk
at the Chinese Cultural Center.*

JO
Oh, a talk, about what?

FONG
*About the development of
Chinese culture in San Francisco.*

JO
Oh...roots, eh? Chinese roots.

FONG
*Yes, yes, yes. People in general
think that Chinese culture is just
something very simple. At most
it's eating.* Such as *eat* Chinese
food. *Actually it's not that
simple. Chinese culture is very
rich and colorful. Like the south
and the north can be
differentiated. And the ancient
and the modern are even more
varied. Right? For example, it's
like in literature one can see that
it's different. As for the north,
you take a look: "The sky is blue,
the land is vast. When the wind*

blows, the grass bends, and I can see cows and sheep." This is a northern scene. In the south, it's different. *"The wind blows, the red silk parts. Turn around for the gentleman to carry."* These are southern sentiments. And in drama it's equally varied. Take those in the north: *"One horse has departed the outskirts of* Syī Lyáng." Northern sentiments. In the south, in Cantonese opera, it's again different. You look: *"When the sun sets, the traveller leaves."* Now, this is marvellous art.

JO

Ah, you're a very good scholar, Mr. Fong.

FONG

Oh, don't be so polite. Hey, you seem to have something on your mind these days. What's the matter?

JO

I want to find a friend. (VO) Mr. Fong didn't come up with the important clue, but he did tell me that to solve the mystery I had to think Chinese...

FONG

...come down to have a chat... drink a cup of tea...

JO (VO)

...He told me the Chinese lantern riddle.

Chinese Character Text
of Scenes in Spoken Chinese

Chinese Character Text of Scene 7, pp. 20-26
7. INT. GOLDEN DRAGON RESTAURANT KITCHEN—DAY

SFX: Henry the cook singing "Fry Me to the Moon"

Dressed in a Samurai Night Fever t-shirt, Henry, speaking primarily in Mandarin, is busily reading orders, mixing sauces, wok-frying, and guzzling milk.

JO (VO)
Steve's joke reminded me of someone Chan Hung talks about a lot. The cook at the Golden Dragon who wears a Samurai Night Fever t-shirt, drinks milk, chain smokes, and sings "Fry Me to the Moon," all while he's cooking up five orders of sweet and sour pork.

HENRY
…什麼？

He picks up an order on a slip of paper.
呵，甜酸排骨三份！他媽的！這臭老美
一天到晚就吃這個，我真不懂，什麼好
吃的嗎？甜酸排骨…他媽的！我那胃酸
…又來了！
He drinks some milk.
嘔，他媽的！

He takes another gulp.

> 這廚房不是人幹的。我告訴你，你剃
> 頭師博也爲錢，圍着椅子轉圓圈。咱
> 們留學生怎麼樣？留學生也爲錢圍着
> 火爐玩鍋鏟！哈哈！他媽的！

CUT TO:

The dining room of the restaurant. Camera POV (point-of-view) is that of a waiter taking orders from patrons. At one table, an older Chinese couple and their daughter discuss their choices, partly in Cantonese.

> DAUGHTER
> What about, what about a—
> 白菜？

> FATHER
> 白菜唔好啦，清炒芥蘭啦，好嗎？

> MOTHER
> 好靭...

> DAUGHTER
> No, I want something with beef
> in it. (to CAM: camera) You have
> something with beef in it?

> MOTHER
> 好肥...

> DAUGHTER
> What about...

> FATHER
> 唔啱燒鴨啦，好嗎？

> MOTHER
> 燒鴨肥...食雞。

> DAUGHTER
> No, that's too heavy, that's too
> heavy for lunch, mom...what
> about fish?

FATHER
(tentatively)

清蒸...清蒸...

DAUGHTER

Yeah, yeah... fish.

FATHER

...石斑。

DAUGHTER

Yeah.

MOTHER

哦，好呀。

DAUGHTER

Yeah, that rock cod sounds good.

CUT TO:

Another table, where a young man hands back a dish of food
to the waiter.

YOUNG MAN (to CAM)

We didn't order this.

The young man shakes his head and turns to the young
woman next to him.

YOUNG WOMAN

...you know, did you see that
movie...

Jo and Steve enter through the front door of the restaurant
and speak to a waitress.

WAITRESS

He's working downstairs in the
kitchen. You want to see him?

JO

Yeah ...唔該 。

WAITRESS

Okay, you go here (pointing) and
go down.

唔該...唔該...

JO

Jo and Steve make their way through the dining room towards the kitchen. We hear snatches of conversation between the young man and woman.

> YOUNG WOMAN
> ...long time...

> YOUNG MAN
> ...long time ago...

> YOUNG WOMAN
> ...that's a good one...but another thing is a...

CUT TO:

Another table, occupied by a white man, a white woman, and across the table two Chinese women, speaking partly in Cantonese, who cannot be seen directly but only via a reflection in the mirror.

> CHINESE WOMAN
> ...眞係麻煩㗎...唔好講...(referring to the white man)
> 漏氣鬼嚟㗎,你眞係! (giggles)

> WHITE WOMAN
> (to white man) What's lauhhei?
> (turns to the Chinese woman)
> What's lauhhei?

> WHITE MAN
> (starts to explain)
> Lauhhei...

> SECOND CHINESE WOMAN
> (squeals)
> Leaking gas!

> WHITE WOMAN
> Leaking what?

WHITE MAN

Lauhhei means...(others are all laughing)...not together, not together; I didn't do it.

CUT TO:

The kitchen, where Jo and Steve listen to Henry the cook.

HENRY

陳雄呵，從小跟我一塊兒，我們倆是同學，一塊兒上大學，上那個航空工程系。在大學裡...aeronautics engineering...哪，他在班裡功課才好啦。老考第一。我考第四十五；全班四十六個學生。哈哈哈！來美國以後怎麼樣？找不到工作，找不到工作你知道吧！沒人要，你沒有什麼辦法。那麼，這些美國人要什麼呢？他不要人給你搞什麼航空工程嘛。他就是要你做什麼蛋卷，egg roll, sweet sour pork, won ton soup, 這些玩藝兒。

He reads an order and responds to Camera/Waiter.

怎麼？　　Five won ton soup
又來了！我跟你講呵，下次老美要來吃這個，你跟他講："We don't have won ton soup, we have won ton soup spelled backwards—'not now!'"
哈哈哈！

Some ingredients are stir-fried in a wok. Henry continues in VO.

他媽的！那會兒攔回去了。
...The funny thing was, the other day he's bussing a table and there came these friends of his, colleagues of his from Taiwan, lives in the United States, in San Francisco. The

minute he saw those friends he
rushed from the back door and
never came back again...

CUT TO:

A table in the dining room, where people, speaking in Cantonese, are fighting over a check—with the only male at the
table managing to get it.

> ### HENRY (VO)
> 中國人嘛，要面子嘛...You know, the
> problem is, I think this guy has
> too much pride, too much pride.

> ### WOMAN AT TABLE
> 係，呢個係...

> ### SECOND WOMAN
> 唔駛你呀。都話...

> ### THIRD WOMAN
> 嘅好意思呀。成日你請...

> ### MAN
> 唔緊要啦。唔緊要。下一次你哋。

> ### FOURTH WOMAN
> 好呀。好呀。

> ### FIFTH WOMAN
> 多謝。

> ### HENRY (VO)
> 我禮拜四休息，跟你打電話...Thursday,
> talk to you later, okay?

> ### JO (VO)
> Okay.

> ### HENRY (VO)
> Bye bye, Jo.

15. EXT. ROOFTOP—DAY (flashback)

Henry the cook, dressed in a three-piece suit, converses with Jo, partly in Mandarin.

SFX: Street traffic; passing Chinese drum and cymbal music.

JO (VO)
Henry thought that Chan Hung went back to China because it was just too difficult for him to identify with the mainland Chinese from 8,000 miles away. That makes Chan Hung out to be too simple. He had a lot more on his mind than that. Chan Hung once told me that he wouldn't go back to China until he had achieved something in America.

HENRY
在美國你要做一個中國人哪。唯一的辦法。你要和 nine hundred... you i—... you have to identify with the nine hundred million Chinese in China...

JO
(interrupting)
Ah, wait a minute—

HENRY
... Then you have, you have some, some meaning there.

JO
Wait a minute. But you know here are, you know we're Chinese here too. There are a lot of Chinese. You're Chinese here too.

HENRY

You are...you know...

在這兒，在在在在美國人家就

把你當外國人看。 You are
foreigners here, you know that.
You don't belong here. People
consider you a foreigner. You're,
you're born here, right?

你...你生＿A.B.C.?

JO

Right.

BOTH
(in unison)

A.B.C.

HENRY

You're A.B.C.

人家把你當為美國人嗎？They still
consider you as a foreigner.

JO

Yeah, I know, but you know—
here, right here, we have to do
something. We have to fight.

HENRY

Fight, fight for what? Fight
for recognition. You know
how long we've been here?

我們來這兒一百多年啦。一百多年，
然後加五十萬中國人在這兒。

Half million Chinese, one hundred
years. If they don't recognize us,
they don't want to recognize us,
and they will not recognize us.
You know what I mean?

我們這一輩子就只過一次。可憐得很
哪。人的一輩子過一次。做點兒有意

義的事。 You...you only live
once. So we should do something
more...more significant. How's
that, eh?

Chinese Character Text of Scene 43, pp. 68-69

43. EXT. PORTSMOUTH SQUARE—DAY

Jo walks up to Mr. Fong, a scholarly-looking man dressed in a
suit. They stand and talk in Cantonese at the edge of the park.

                    FONG
    ...唔見好耐。你好嗎？

                    JO
    好...好...你去邊度呀？

                    FONG
    我啱啱喺中國文化中心去演講返嚟呀嘛。

                    JO
    哦，演講，講乜嘢呀？

                    FONG
    講中國文化喺三藩市嘅發展。

                    JO
    Oh...roots, eh? Chinese roots.

                    FONG
    係，係，係。一般人呢，以為中國文化呢
    ，就係一個好簡單嘅。最多係食呀。
    Eat Chinese food 呀咁囉。其實唔係咁
    簡單嘅。中國文化呢，係好豐富多彩嘅。
    南北都有得分別嘅。古今就更加唔同啦。
    係嘛？譬如好似文學上表現出嚟就唔一樣
    。北方嘅，你睇吓：「 天蒼蒼，野茫茫。
    風吹草低見牛羊。」呢個係北國嘅風光。
    喺南方就唔同個囉吓。「 風吹紅羅裂，轉
    身就郎抱。」呢啲係南方嘅情調。喺戲劇
    上邊一樣係唔同。佢北方嗰啲呢：「一馬
    離了，西涼界。」北國嘅情調。喺南方呢
    ，粵劇裏頭呢，又唔同囉吓和。你睇：「 夕
    陽斜照，離人去。」啲呢啲好奇藝嘅。

                    JO
    Ah, you're a very good scholar,
    Mr. Fong.

FONG

哦，駛乜咁客氣喇。喂，你呢排都好似
有啲心事咁。有乜嘢事呀？

JO

我想揾個朋友呀。(VO) Mr. Fong
didn't come up with the
important clue, but he did tell me
that to solve the mystery I had to
think Chinese...

FONG

...落吓嚟傾吓偈啦...飲杯茶啦...

JO (VO)

...He told me the Chinese
lantern riddle.

Interview with Wayne Wang

Diane Mark: Tell me how you first became interested in making films.

Wayne Wang: Well, I grew up with a lot of films. My dad was a real film buff, so we used to go to at least two to three movies a week. Then I went to art school, and basically majored in painting and photography for a while, all the time wanting to get involved in films, but I wanted to have a more basic education in art first. And then after that, in graduate school, I decided to start making films. So I think it's always been there. It's always been a very strong force, movies. All the games that I used to play with my brothers were from movies that we'd seen or play-acting movies and things like that.

DM: Do you remember anything in particular?

WW: Well, cowboys and Indians, good guys and bad guys, spy movies. We recreated a lot of stories from movies that we saw.

DM: Is it true that you were named after John Wayne?

WW: Yeah. But there's more to that story. Usually people just print that part of it. But the story is actually much more interesting because when my father was born, in those days they still would take the kid to a fortune teller. Fortune teller would suggest names based on palm reading and face readings. And the fortune teller told my grandfather that my father would not have enough wood in his life. Wood is one of the key elements. So my grandfather gave my father the name "King of the Forest," because the two characters for forest are made up of five wood characters. So his whole name is all wood. Okay, then the first-born, my older brother came along, and he was named "Prince of the Forest." And then I came along—by that time my parents were westernized, my dad was a great film buff, a fan of John Wayne, so I got named Wayne. And my Chinese name actually came from the English romanization.

DM: That's unusual.

WW: Uh huh. So they completely reversed that process.

DM: What is your Chinese name?

WW: Wing. It means a bud, something that's blossoming, basically that, I think.

DM: Your background in Hong Kong. What schools did you go to, what were some of your early kinds of interests? I just saw a movie called "Father and Son," made in Hong Kong by Alan Fong. The son wanted to make films but the father had other plans for him, and I'm just wondering if you see any parallels to your boyhood in Hong Kong.

WW: Not to "Father and Son." My father wanted me to be in business. My father was interested in films, but not as a career for me. But I've always been on the fringe of academics, so to speak. All through high school, I was involved with a lot of plays, involved with a lot of extracurricular activities as related to that.

DM: Were you acting or on the other end?

WW: I was acting. I did acting, I did a lot of verse speaking and I was very good at that. I won a lot of prizes. In Hong Kong there's this thing called the Music Festival every year, and they have a lot of events like singing and verse speaking. Verse speaking is really reciting poetry, like very old, classic British stuff. And that sort of helped me in that whole area of acting, and eventually, getting involved in films.

DM: Have you heard much reaction from your family, to "Chan is Missing?"

WW: Yeah, they like it a lot, especially my dad, who was in New York when the film opened at the New Directors. He was really impressed and proud. Before, he had conflicting feelings about my involvement with film, because most of the earlier films I'd done were in a sense experimental, and he didn't see what those films were doing, for me as a career, and also the value of them in terms of audience. So "Chan is Missing" is the first one that broke through all that. I think he was pretty happy about that.

DM: Getting back to your coming to the U.S., you came primarily for school?

WW: Yeah, actually I came over here for college. Went to Foothill for a year or so and then went to California College of Arts and Crafts, and pretty much stayed there til I got my masters.

DM: You've been living in the Bay Area for how long now?

WW: Since 1969. Well, Los Altos is probably the Bay Area too, so 1967. San Francisco and Berkeley area since 1969.

DM: So you were around during that real colorful period.

WW: During the strikes and the Telegraph Avenue stuff and all that? Yes.

DM: Did you participate in any of that? The strikes, the demos?

WW: Some of it, not that directly. I remember during the Vietnam war, at Arts and Crafts, we did a lot of posters. A lot of the anti-war posters were made through the school. So all of us helped out and did that. I was never quite directly involved with all the Berkeley stuff since I wasn't a student at Berkeley. I was also living with a family that was very radical in some ways, a lot of draft resistance work, but was not, you know, really directly involved in a lot of things.

DM: Now, what made you get involved in Chinatown?

WW: It's a long answer. There were a lot of things. Although I wasn't directly involved in a lot of the demonstrations and strikes at that time, I think there were a lot of indirect influences in what I found was important about how I should live and how things should be around me. And also going back to Hong Kong, there were a lot of reactions about the economics of Hong Kong and kind of a helpless feeling about being able to do anything there. And coming back here and seeing conditions in Chinatown, seeing all these new immigrants come in, needing help, not quite getting the help, and getting not only economically depressed, but psychologically and emotionally, too. So I decided to just work in Chinatown in a very real, practical way. To just help people. That's how I initially got involved. Because I was pretty idealistic and I didn't want to deal with things that were just intellectual. I stuck with very practical things.

DM: What year was this?

WW: I think that was in '73, '74, somewhere around '74. I started teaching English, then I started teaching English related to helping people get jobs, then I became more of an administrator in a community agency that did that. I was involved with a lot of community college-type classes, and also involved with a cultural organization called Xin Feng She, which is mainly a community organization with people from all ages, teaching people Mandarin, having parties together, singing, putting on plays. Xin Feng She means "New Wind."

DM: You went back to Hong Kong when you graduated, and worked there in television?

WW: In a TV studio, right. And also did some commercial work, as an assistant director, pretty much in the business end of it. I was a little frustrated about that, I mean I was pretty idealistic about the kinds of films I wanted to do and all that, so I didn't quite fit in very well. That's why when I came back I didn't want to get involved with working with TV studios or working in the whole film *business* at that time. And so I was gonna make my own films outside of the industry, so to speak, and then just work in a lot of community projects.

DM: You made, when you got back here, a couple of films before "Chan is Missing." One was experimental?

WW: Right. One was called "New Relationships." That was the main one, I think. I also did some TV work that was related to Chinatown. I did a program called "Wah Kue." The movie "New Relationships" was all constructed pretty much before I shot it, on paper, and a lot of it was just anima- tion table stuff, very little live footage. So, it was the kind of film that you could sort of all put together in your head, and then just shoot it. It's not a drama kind of a film, but it's very theoretical in a lot of ways. And it's l-ong. I did that film to just sort of get it out of my system, but I felt that I was still doing something in film. And doing something that was to- tally within my limits, where I didn't have to depend on a big cast or crew, or a lot of equipment, so I could do everything very slowly on my own.

DM: How did you fund it?

WW: With my own salary.

DM: And "Wah Kue" was done in conjunction with a studio here?

WW: Yeah, with a TV studio called KRON TV. It was a public affairs show. And I helped Loni (Ding) a little bit on "Bean Sprouts" and, oh, different people who were doing projects around here.

DM: Now, "Chan is Missing." When did the seed first appear?

WW: Well, it first appeared more as a semi-documentary, focusing on cab drivers. Two of them happened to be Chinese. I wrote that proposal to American Film Institute, and after I got the grant, it sort of like grew from that to more. That's why certain elements of it still exist, the somewhat documen- tary aspect of it and also the two cab drivers are remnants of the original seed of "Chan is Missing." And in the mean- time, the process went through a lot of changes. It swung back and forth between a lot of different things that came up. At one point it became very experimental and structural, but I took it away from that after I sat down with some of the crew and cast and realized that I didn't want to make another film that was real theoretical, real experimental and just sat on the shelf more than it was getting shown. So, we made a lot of adjustments and pulled it back towards what it is today.

DM: One reviewer quoted you as saying that you thought it was an "extremely compromised" movie. Do you remember the context?

WW: Yeah, I don't know if I used "extremely" compromised. It *is* compromised.

DM: Are you happy with the way it ended up?

WW: Yeah. I knew that that was what it was going to be. And I think at that time, like I said, I wanted a film that would reach a broader audience, that could communicate on less esoteric grounds. At the time I was writing science curriculum for kids. That was a very interesting experience because trying to talk to kids, trying to communicate to kids, and help kids learn science was a very good, actually, insight into making "Chan is Missing." A lot of the decisions were influenced by that. That's why I always sort of believed that even though I did community work, a lot of that community work was much more important than what I learned in film school. A lot of working as an administrator helps me today in terms of my organizational skills, dealing with people, and so forth. I think that in any field that you work in, a lot of the skills are transferable. And so, writing curriculum for kids was a very key part in what I think "Chan" eventually became. Presenting basically very abstract, intellectual ideas that I'm interested in and trying to communicate it at a very broad level. So a lot of the premise of "Chan is Missing" came out of that.

DM: Content-wise, the film "Chan is Missing" is so refreshing because there's such a good understanding of the community, and I think it does stem from your active involvement.

WW: Well, the film couldn't have been made unless I spent all those years there.

DM: Are some of the incidents taken from actual things that happened?

WW: I think almost all of them. Chan is really a composite of a lot of people. Part of it is probably me, part of it is my brother, part of it are people that I've worked with in the agency. So there's a little bit of everything in Chan.

DM: Chan the movie?

WW: Yeah. Right. Chan the character in the film, too. When people say Chan Hung is sort of a metaphor for Chinatown, in some ways it's really true, because Chan Hung is really a character who was a blank page that a lot of incidences or a lot of different parts of different people in Chinatown with similar experiences could be painted into. Even the people in the community itself sort of all painted their own version of him.

DM: The time schedule for the making of "Chan." What was that like?

WW: Let's see. I think it was '79 that I got the grant. We didn't start filming the thing until '80. And got it done by '81. It was distributed in '82. So actually it all started in '79, late '79.

DM: How long did it take you to get your script together?

WW: The script was in a completely different form. Like I said, it was very structural at one time. It took a couple of months to get that together. Three months I think. Then we changed a lot of things on that. And that took maybe about a month or so. We took some of the script from the other more structural one, kept parts of it, and then rewrote some sections. And it went in with a lot of the dialogue not in, but having a real clear idea as to what we wanted to do with it. For example, George with the apple pie. Because I'd heard him say that story a lot. So it'd be like, well, George will tell his apple pie story to illustrate Chinese Americanism, blah blah. So the script itself, when we went into shooting, had a whole range of things. Some scenes were very well written out, like the lawyer scene, where she explains the traffic accident. Except the actors then embellished it, played around with it even more. To scenes like, we'd say, George is gonna tell his apple pie stories, to other scenes to which Woody and Marc contributed a lot, when we'd sit down and say, well, this is where we want to get to, this is the purpose, and these are some of the points. Let's talk it through a little bit. So there was a whole spectrum of different kinds of approaches.

DM: How well scripted out was the pier scene?

WW: Oh, the pier scene was scripted out kind of medium-rough. Now, I scripted it out and gave it a few days before we shot it to Woody and Marc. We never rehearsed it. I went through telling them exactly what the main points were, the sequence of the points. And what they did was to read through it, and then when we shot it, since they understood the whole time sequence of the scene, and what had happened and all of that, they could play around with it. So that's pretty much how we went in on that scene. In certain scenes where we rehearsed it, Marc was very good. Marc knew his lines very well. But Marc, you know, if we didn't rehearse it and sort of went in on it, he would sort of just, you know, make up a lot of things. Which is really strong, too. So I wanted to use a little bit of both. So in that pier scene, I wanted to work with the best of both worlds, where both Marc and Woody could improvise somewhat, and yet be real clear on what the points were, and where we wanted to get to. So we basically shot, I think three different takes straight through. It gave us some leeway to intercut between the three takes.

DM: Okay, one more question about the writing process. There are three people credited. What was the writing process involved and how did you collaborate?

WW: Well, I think Danny Yung and I worked on the original, original version, which was the more structural version. And then, Terrel (Seltzer) and I worked on the next version, which was more narrative and story-oriented. Terrel worked out some of the dialogue. Then we brought in the actors and they helped fill in a lot more. Isaac (Cronin) came in after the film was shot and helped me work on a lot of the narration.

DM: Directing, producing, editing. Do you have a favorite at this stage?

WW: They all sort of go hand in hand. I think my favorite out of the three is editing. That's where a lot of the material actually gets honed down. You can really see, you can really manipulate, because everything is there, everything is all physical. So I like that the best. Although they all go hand in hand. You can't edit until you have certain materials, which is the directing stage, and you can't direct unless it's produced with certain insight, so I think they're all pretty connected.

DM: You said that you wanted to encourage other Asian American filmmakers through the making of this movie. Can you expound on that a bit?

WW: I really believe that too many people talk about wanting to make films, and they think too big. They always think like these million dollar movies. They'll never get to make them. I think that what's more important, particularly at this stage, if you have a vision and if you have strong creative ideas, put them down on paper. They don't have to be that proficient. You don't have to make a film that's totally professional, and technically perfect. Put down your ideas even though it's rough. You work with the roughness, and make it work for you. I've always believed in that, and I still do, to a certain extent, particularly for Asian American film-makers, because if everyone is gonna wait around to get their big money, if everyone is gonna wait around for their funding, you know, like one film is gonna come out every three or four years. I mean we've been at it since the sixties trying to make these films. I think more things should come out, whether they're perfect or not. I mean, it takes time, I worked with it. So that's the strong thing, I think the strongest thing about "Chan is Missing" is that, I feel. Is that, there was a commitment from all of us involved to just do it. And not worry, and say wait, we don't have enough lights, it's not gonna look right, but we said, well, you know, let's work with it. Let's do the best we can. Make our ideas work. And I think the result of it was something very interesting and people at least accepted it, and it did well. Got more exposure than any other Asian American film that came along. And hopefully there'll be more of it. You know, even if you have to shoot in videotape, shoot in videotape. Transfer it to film. There's a new film that just came out called "Signal Seven" which I think is going to be a very interesting film. It's done in, again, very low budget, shot in 3/4″ video and blown up to 35. And apparently it looks decent.

DM: Now, you shot black and white, as a case in point in this discussion. How did you deal with equipment?

WW: Well, we rented equipment. Very limited stuff. Michael Chin the cameraman had his own lights and we rented other ones. You know, whatever we could. Some of the equipment we rented from friends who gave it to us at very low rates. So there was a lot of that going on. $20,000 for a feature is very low. I wouldn't want to try that low again, unless it's something much more controlled. But anywhere between $20,000 and $50,000. Actually, Michael and I were working on some budgets. $35,000—it's reasonable. We would attempt another one at $35,000. I think we could get some good quality out of that.

DM: Does that include crew salaries and actor's fees?

WW: Some. Very basic.

DM: People would still keep their day jobs, right?

WW: Right!

DM: You have a dedication to Wong Cheen in the film credits. Who is this person?

WW: Oh, just, I think it's more of an abstract person. (laughs)

DM: Male or female abstract? (laughing)

WW: Could be both!

DM: Oh, very interesting. Just happened to like the name or something?

WW: Yeah, just sort of—(laughing)

DM: That's all you care to say about that?

WW: Yeah.

DM: Okay. Moving right along—

WW: It's like Chan, you know.

DM: Chan's sister?

WW: Yeah, that's right.

DM: There are sections where it's all purely spoken in Chinese. Did you entertain the thought of going with English subtitles?

WW: At one time, yeah. And then I remember a reviewer saw it and had an interesting response, which I thought was quite valid. It was that he said it was more interesting, actually, trying to guess at what's going on. And I sort of believe in that, in that I think you don't need to know specifically what's going on at any given time. You can sort of like, let the film work with you on a more organic and emotional level. And so I don't think everything needs to be subtitled. To get people used to hearing a foreign language is very important. We're trying some of that with "Dim Sum" [Wang's next film] again, although some of the stuff in "Dim Sum" will have to be subtitled. Some of it we don't. Like what Peter [the fry cook in "Chan"] was doing, saying things in Chinese and English, is a really interesting aspect.

DM: That's really, I don't know if it would be Chinese American, but it's really Chinese-in-America for the character to be talking like that.

WW: Yeah. And also the whole idea that this person speaks all in Chinese and then Jo would talk about it from his own perspective, so you're never quite sure whether you're hearing really what is being said. And I think it's important. Because the whole film is really about interpretations, and words, what do they mean? Because at the end, Jo says, "The problem with me is I believe what I see and hear." Should you do that, you know?

DM: Why did you include both Mandarin and Cantonese?

WW: Well, because I think that's true, particularly in New York, San Francisco, and L.A. Immigrants are not just Cantonese- or Toisan-speaking. There's all those different dialects. A lot of immigrants are Mandarin-speaking.

DM: How and where did you find your actors?

WW: Well, let's see. The key professional people are all from the Asian American Theater workshop. And most of the other people were just friends or people that I knew in the community.

DM: Who were the people from the Theater Workshop?

WW: Wood Moy, Marc Hayashi, Judy Nihei, and Emily Yamasaki. And then all the others were pretty much just friends or people from the community that I've known. During the process of putting together the film, I'd see them and say, oh yeah, he would be an interesting character, he's a real ham. We used a lot of people like that. Or somebody like Frankie, who literally walked into our movie. While we were setting up, he just walked in, and said, "Oh, I know this guy," and he just walks right into the set and starts talking. Yeah. And he's a real character that way, anyway.

DM: That must have been a real interesting exercise for you as a director, to try to get an even tone out of a scene that involved both professionals and non-professionals.

WW: Yeah it is. Well, it wasn't that hard because both Woody and Marc both felt comfortable playing very realistic, felt comfortable improvising somewhat. They didn't always need a script all the time. Because of that, it made it a lot easier. We tried the same thing with "Dim Sum," and it was a more interesting problem, mainly it was more scripted, and also keeping some of that quality of improvising too. We were also using very, very professional people with totally non-professionals, and it's an interesting chemistry that worked in there.

DM: In terms of the acting in "Chan," were you pleased with any people or sections in particular?

WW: I liked a lot of the later stuff that we shot. Scenes between Marc and Woody, like the scene between the two of them in the car, talking about the riddle. The scene between Marc and Woody outside the car, talking about the Chicanos fighting the Filipinos. A lot of the badgering back and forth between Woody and Marc. Because by that time, they'd developed a relationship, and we all felt more comfortable working with them. Their characters became more clear for all of us, and I think it really developed nicely. I liked a lot of that.

DM: Your shooting took place over how many weeks?

WW: Well, it took place over ten weeks. And then we went into the editing room for a while, and picked up one weekend of shooting later on. A lot of that stuff was also done in that last weekend.

DM: But the ten weeks were—

WW: Weekends. Saturday, Sunday, and then stop. Saturday, Sunday, stop.

DM: Are there dolly shots in this film?

WW: There's one, in a wheelchair! It was actually quite an elaborate dolly shot that got cut up because it just played too long. The one where it starts off with a shot from the inside looking out, where they're talking to Mrs. Chan, and then they come in through the door, and then it swings around and all this. It was a much more elaborate dolly shot which didn't completely play as one long shot. That was the only dolly shot we did. There was a lot of hand-held stuff.

DM: Do things like Chinese art and painting, something

that might have stemmed from your background, influence the way you shot or sculpted the film? The use of space, etc.

WW: Not really. The original script, the one I said was more structural, had a lot more of that. But then when we shifted to this one, and because of the limitations, I don't think we really could afford to do this very elaborate, aesthetic kind of thing about Chinese art and everything. The only thing is maybe there is this whole idea of the negative space, and not only in terms of Chan's character, you know how in the end he's a negative character, that he never appeared on the screen and all that. The way it was shot there was some of that, like Woody driving and his face is all blocked out, then he appears and buildings appear across the windshield. Other than that, compositionally and aesthetically, I don't think it had a whole lot of the theoretical concepts I've always been interested in. The original, structural idea about "Chan is Missing" which is based actually on the development of the Chinese written character. But that all got dropped.

DM: The development of the Chinese written character?

WW: Basically, the original concept when it was more structural was that the development of the Chinese written character is quite interesting because it parallels the development of film history. Eisenstein's theory of film history. And we wanted to make a film that was structured after the four basic stages of the development of the Chinese written character. That's very theoretical in some ways. But that'll come back one of these days. And I have a lot of interesting concepts about how Chinese paintings or poetry would apply to films. I don't know whether we'd want to get into that here, because it's sort of a separate issue. In "Dim Sum," we initially tried to do some of it again, but realized that for very practical reasons we couldn't afford to. In "Dim Sum," there's more of it, there's much more of it.

DM: That shot that you love, of the ocean. Where does that come from?

WW: That comes from, actually, just paintings that I used to do, and paintings that I used to like. There was a guy who used to draw water, in black and white. The water comes from a painter, a British painter who did a lot of water, and I've always liked it and I used it. The reason I like it is that it's so simple and direct. And the flatness of that image, where foreground background becomes one. You know, there's no right side up, you can turn that image any way and it's all still the same. The light and darkness is also ambiguous. An image that also changes, has its own rhythm, fills the whole screen. So there are a lot of aspects that have always fascinated me. It's a perfect sort of visual metaphor for what's going on with the Chan character.

DM: The fact that there's no solution at the end of the film, and the summary, Jo's voiceover—can you discuss that a little bit?

WW: Part of that came out of writing the curriculum for kids. Writing science curriculum, which is very solution-bound. And at the time we were writing the curriculum, we were exploring the possibility of so-called more Asian-oriented science, and what that really means. Which led me to the idea that (this would cause a lot of discussion but I think it's an interesting starting point) Asians tend to have a much higher tolerance for ambiguity, and have always historically been able to deal with ambiguity a lot more than so-called Caucasian minds, or Western minds. And I think that the ability, the dual ability of being able to be very obsessive about solutions and at the same time being able to accept ambiguity, is very important for the future development of science and thinking. And that also stems back to this whole thing about bilingual and bicultural thinking. So that's why the film really deals with being very specific, looking for solutions, looking for answers, and yet at the same time the acceptance of ambiguity. So at that level I think there were a lot of things going on there that, you know, some people got into, some people didn't. But I felt it was important that at the end of the film, you didn't find Chan, that you never see him. That's the only way I think the movie *could* end.

DM: How did you choose the name Chan?

WW: Because it's a common last name, and also because of Charlie Chan.

DM: And the no-solution thing also seems to be a direct contradiction to the Charlie Chan mode, where there's always a solution, and he ties it up real neatly.

WW: Right. I think that people look for easy answers all the time, particularly in more commercial films. And I think that's a bad thing. I think films can be a lot more open-ended, that people can be more creative in their own ways of finding answers.

DM: Do you consider this an ABC or an FOB film?

WW: It's sort of like a bastard child of both. That's something for me, too. I think it's a new kind of animal or creation that's really a product of being both FOB and also ABC. I wasn't born here, so I can't say I'm totally ABC, but I've gone through some of the similar experiences, understand some of the experiences that ABCs have gone through. Yet I'm really an FOB, so I've got parts of both. But I'm not totally an FOB anymore either.

DM: Contemporary Hong Kong filmmaking. Do you identify with anything that's happening back there?

WW: Yeah, there's a lot. Like Alan Fong's films I like a lot.

DM: What are the trends that are happening?

WW: Well I think the trends are that there are a lot of young directors that have studied here, or in Europe, and have gone back to Hong Kong. Because Hong Kong is such a commercial market, they have to first deal with that. Deal with a very mass audience. And through that, try to do work that has more integrity, is more interesting, has conceptual ideas behind it. And it's been taking a long time, but it's all coming out. Ann Hui is one director who has done some interesting work. "Boat People" is going to be in the New York Film Festival this year. It straddles a really mass-oriented film with something more than that. Dealing with their own culture of Hong Kong. Clifford Choy, who used to work out of here and now has gone back, has made a film with the Shaw Brothers called "Hong Kong, Hong Kong" that I hear is very interesting. Alan Fong is unique in Hong Kong in that he refused to deal with the commercial aspects, made "Father and Son," which did very well at the box office, and continues to make his "family dramas." So there are a lot of these different elements that are coming out. I think the commonality is that they all work with the mass audience and yet try to go beyond that, and work with more *ideas,* work with Hong Kong, being very bicultural in Hong Kong ways. So, I think they're very strong films. In the next ten years there are gonna be many more films from our generation of filmmakers that have gone back.

DM: Are you yourself interested in shooting something there?

WW: Yeah. I've got an idea that I really want to do, which takes place half in San Francisco and half in Hong Kong. It's relating both, in some ways. And it's a horror film.

DM: We're wondering if "Chan is Missing" was also influenced by some of the Western drama that's come out. By Western I mean, Asian American, theater—David Henry Hwang's plays, etc.

WW: Not specifically related to any particular one, but more just a general sense of watching a lot of plays at Asian American Theater Workshop. More in terms of a way of expressing what it means to be Chinese American, the frustrations, without falling into the trap of always complaining that because of racism we've been mistreated. I think it's more seeing the need to express what our experiences are, without falling into the trap of being the crybaby. In a more general sense, that's sort of the influence of all of that. And that's a very personal thing on my part. I'm not saying that whatever other things that deal with the railroad workers or historical pieces are not important. They're just as important. It's just that for my own sensibility, I didn't want to come off doing that.

DM: Why are the white people in the film portrayed as they are?

WW: Are there any white people in the film? (laughing)

DM: (laughing) Yeah, a couple slipped in. They must have been walking past the set. Took a seat at the restaurant table.

WW: Right. Because it seems like for white people, in a very broad sense, their only relationship with Chinatown is going there to eat. Then there's one character who understands some Chinese. There's the kind that want to be Asian, that they should have been born Asian, but they're not. Other than that, are there any more?

DM: The tourist in the cab.

WW: Right. It seems that in terms of "Chan is Missing," that's really their relationship to all that's going on. I think as you show what Chinatown is, without showing the outside mainstream society, you say a lot about the mainstream also. Like why can't Chan get a job? Is there a historical relationship to all of that, things like that you can sort of get a sense of? So the product of Chinatown is indirectly in relationship to the mainstream society around it also.

DM: What did you learn from the making of "Chan" that might be passed on as advice to young filmmakers, especially Asian Americans?

WW: I guess what we said earlier, which is not to wait around for the big bucks, just go out and do it, with whatever resources that you have, even if it's just credit cards. As long as there's a strong idea, and people are committed, just do it. I want to go back to doing that some more, too.

DM: What is it you want to go back to?

WW: Oh, shooting a film on a very low budget. Even though now I can afford not to. I mean, it's too easy to try to protect what I have and say, "Well, I can't do this anymore." But I feel like I want to go back, maybe, like $35-50,000 range shoot a film that's all hand-held with very little lights, very rough film. The other thing from "Chan" is how to make the limitations work for you, rather than work against you. That takes a lot of experience. You just can't, you know, say, well I'm gonna make a film and just do that. I think you need to know what the pitfalls are, how much you can push your resources and work within them, and make them work for you. That's a very key thing.

DM: What to *you* constitutes a successful film?

WW: For me it's pretty much, I don't know, that's a tough question. I guess for me it's really when you have a story or a concept that you really believe in, and if you try to figure out a way of presenting it in the strongest way possible, and do your best to make it work within, again, all your limited resources—and get it done. People are not aware of how difficult it is to finish a film. I mean, years ago I thought, god, at least I've made one feature film. This was even before "Chan" came out. And how difficult that whole process was, to just finish a film. I think a film is successful as long as you finish it. I can get real critical about a lot of things on it, there will always be problems and areas where you never quite achieve what you really want to do. I think finishing itself is a great accomplishment. The rest of it you just sort of let the audience decide.

Selected Bibliography of Reviews

"Acclaimed Film to Be Shown at Art Academy," *Honolulu Star-Bulletin,* June 17, 1982.

Accomando, Beth, "'Chan'—Low Budget Film Reveals Young Talent," *La Jolla, Cal. Light,* Aug. 26, 1982.

Ansen, David, "Chinese Puzzle," *Newsweek,* June 21, 1982.

Archibald, Lewis, "You Probably Won't Go See This Because It Isn't A Middle American Whomp And Stomp Movie. But Maybe You Should," *The Aquarian/Manhattan,* June 9-16, 1982.

Aufderheide, Pat, "The Mystery of the Missing Identity," *In These Times,* June 16-29, 1982.

Baltake, Joe, "Chan is Missing," *Philadelphia Daily News,* Sept. 3, 1982.

Boyce, Terry, "Director's Profile: Wayne Wang," *Studio One,* Hong Kong, July 1982.

Canby, Vincent, "Unexpected Dividends At a Festival," *The New York Times,* May 2, 1982.

Canby, Vincent, "Film: 'Chan is Missing' in Chinatown," *The New York Times,* April 24, 1982.

Chan, Maxine, "Wayne Wang, Finding Artistic Freedom," *The International Examiner,* Aug. 18, 1982.

Chiu, Tony, "Wayne Wang—He Made the Year's Unlikeliest Hit," *The New York Times,* May 30, 1982.

Cohn, Lawrence, "'Trek II' Hits B'Way, $2.2-Mil; 'Poltergeist' $1.5-Mil; 'Rocky III' Smashing $2.3-Mil; 'Chan' Pow," *Variety,* June 9, 1982.

Crist, Judith, WOR—TV, New York, June 4, 1982.

Cunningham, Dennis, WCBS-TV, New York, June 16, 1982.

Denby, David, "Movies," *New York,* June 7, 1982.

Dittus, Erick, "A Candid Interview with Wayne Wang," *East Village Eye,* July 1982.

Ebert, Roger, "'Chan is Missing' Journeys through Real Chinatown," *Chicago Sun-Times,* Sept. 10, 1982.

Ebert, Roger, "'Chan is Missing' Warm Funny Look at Chinese in U.S.," *Chicago Sun Times,* April 30, 1982.

Feeney, F.X., "Chan is Missing/FILMEX: The Best & The Rest/A Guide to The Film Festival," *L.A. Weekly* March 19-25, 1982.

Feeney, F.X., "A Walking Collision of Cultures: A Conversation with Wayne Wang," *L.A. Weekly,* Aug. 27-Sept. 2, 1982.

Filmex Review, "Chan is Missing," *Variety,* March 19, 1982.

Frymer, Murray, "A Man Who Loves B Movies Wins Fame, Critical Success," Knight-Ridder News Service, Sept. 6, 1982.

Gee, Bill, "Wayne Wang's 'Chan' Suggests Far More Than It States," *Sampan,* July 1982.

Gelmis, Joseph, "'Chan is Missing'; So Are the Cliches," *Newsday,* May 2, 1982.

Gelmis, Joseph, "Movie Reviews/Chan is Missing," *Newsday,* April 23, 1982.

Guthmann, Edward, "Goodbye Stereotypes," *San Francisco Bay Guardian,* July 14, 1982.

Harada, Wayne, "CHAN IS MISSING: A Real Fortune Cookie, With Hidden Messages," *The Honolulu Advertiser,* June 21, 1982.

Harada, Wayne, "Taking a Chan-ce on the Chinese Identity Issue," *The Honolulu Advertiser,* June 29, 1982.

Hatch, Robert, "FILMS," *The Nation,* July 3, 1982.

Iki, John, "'Chan is Missing' Dispels Stereotypes of Asians," *Asian Pacific Lifeline,* Sept. 1982.

Jacobs, Tom, "Low-Budget 'Chan' Entertains, Informs," *Albuquerque, N.M. Journal,* Nov. 19, 1982.

Kishi, Yoshio, "'Chan is Missing' Film Reviewed," *The New York Nichibei,* May 6, 1983.

Kauffman, Stanley, "Stanley Kauffmann on Films," *The New Republic,* June 16, 1982.

Lam, Michael, "Chan is Missing: Hard-Edged, Gutsy," *East/ West,* Dec. 2, 1981.

Lasky, Michael, "Chan is Missing/Chinatown Found," *Bay Area Reporter,* July 8, 1982.

Lau, Alan Chong, "State of the Art/CHAN IS MISSING," *The International Examiner,* July 21, 1982.

Leogrande, Ernest, "'Chan is Missing' An Oriental Puzzle," *The New York Post,* June 4, 1982.

Letner, Ken, "'Chan': An Oriental 'Godot'," *Press-Telegram,* Long Beach, Aug. 13, 1982.

Lum, Wing Tek, "Chan is Missing Marks New Age of Asian American Film," *East/West,* July 28, 1982. Reprinted in *Bamboo Ridge,* No. 17, Dec. 1982-Feb. 1983.

Lyons, Jeffrey, Newsradio 88, New York, June 6, 1982.

Movie Views & Reviews, *US,* July 20, 1982.

O'Toole, Lawrence, "Chinese Translations," *MacLeans,* Toronto, Canada, Sept. 6, 1982.

Olten, Carol, "'Chan' is Low Budget...High Quality," *The San Diego Union,* Aug. 19, 1982.

Picks & Pans/Screen," *People,* July 26, 1982.

Rea, Steven X., "A Fascinating Mystery But 'Chan' is Missing a Solution," *Philadelphia Inquirer,* Sept. 6, 1982.

Rickey, Carrie, "Some Moving Pictures (and Some That Aren't)," *Village Voice,* April 27, 1982.

Siegel, Joel, Eyewitness News, WABC-TV, New York, June 8, 1982.

Silverman, Stephen M., "The Serious Laughs of 'Chan's' Wayne Wang," *New York Post,* June 14, 1982.

Siskel, Gene, "'Chan' Reflects Life, Not Stereotypes," *Chicago Tribune,* Sept. 10, 1982.

Siskel, Gene and Ebert, Roger, "Sneak Previews," PBS, July 1, 1982.

Springer, Richard, "Chan is Missing Breaks Away from the Stereotypical Image," *East/West,* Sept. 23, 1982.

Steritt, David, "Lively, Enriching Tale of the Chinese-American Experience," *The Christian Science Monitor,* July 1, 1982.

Stevens, Dale, "Low-Budget 'Chan' Engaging Film," *The Cincinnati Post,* Nov. 20, 1982.

Stone, Judy, "Chan is Missing'/A Funny, High-Spirited Treat," *San Francisco Chronicle,* July 9, 1982.

Stone, Judy, "A Humorous Treat From Chinatown," *San Francisco Chronicle,* Dec. 12, 1981.

Stoop, Norma McLain, *After Dark*/The Magazine of Entertainment, New York, June 1982.

Sullivan, Tom, "'Chan is Missing' is Sloppy," *The Herald-News,* New Jersey, June 4, 1982.

Tajima, Renee and Lew, Walter, "An Interview with Wayne Wang," program guide, 1982 Asian American International Film Festival.

Thomas, Bob, "'Chan is Missing': A Low-Budget Winner," *Dallas Times Herald,* Aug. 12, 1982.

Thomas, Kevin, "'Chan is Missing,' But Not Talent," *Los Angeles Times,* Aug. 13, 1982.

"This Wang is a Moviemaker," Associated Press release, *Herald American,* Boston, July 30, 1982.

Vadeboncoeur, Joan, "'Chan' a Modest But Well Done Movie," *Syracuse Herald Journal,* Nov. 19, 1982.

Verniere, James, "An Interview with Wayne Wang, Director of 'Chan is Missing'/Racial Categories Are Nonimperative," *The Aquarian/Manhattan,* June 16-23, 1982.

Winsten, Archer, "'Chan is Missing' An Oriental Puzzle," *The New York Post,* June 4, 1982.

Wong, Wayman, "A Mystery Movie is Actually Much More," *San Francisco Examiner,* Dec. 10, 1981.

Woo, Elaine, "His Bargain-Basement Movie is a Surprise Hit," *Los Angeles Herald Examiner,* July 29, 1982.

Zailian, Marian, "A Local's Shoestring Film Stuns the Critics," *San Francisco Sunday Examiner & Chronicle,* July 4, 1982.

photo by Nancy Wong

Wayne Wang

Wayne Wang is an independent producer/director/writer presently based in San Francisco. He captured the attention of the film world in the spring of 1982 with his low-budget black-and-white feature *Chan is Missing*. Hollywood's *Variety* claimed, "*Chan is Missing* is the sort of film that justifies film festivals and makes them essential...Any filmmaker who can so thoroughly force the viewer to look at the world through his eyes possesses a talent to reckon with." Critics throughout the country sent equal praise to press.

Born and raised in Hong Kong, Wang came to the United States in the late 1960s for college. He has a B.F.A. in Painting and an M.F.A. in Film and Television from the California College of Arts and Crafts. He was producer/director for *Wah Kue—The Chinese in America*, KRON-Television, San Francisco, and director of *Below the Lion Rock*, a Hong Kong

Government Film/Television Unit weekly television series. His photography and films have been exhibited internationally. Following *Chan is Missing,* Wang directed *Dim Sum,* a feature film about five Asian American women tackling the strains of everyday life, a film eagerly anticipated by critics and audiences alike.

Diane Mei Lin Mark

Diane Mei Lin Mark is a writer who has been active in Asian American concerns for over a decade. She has worked as a staff reporter for *The Honolulu Advertiser,* an oral history researcher, and a writer and associate producer/director for the Asian American film series *Pearls,* aired nationwide on PBS in 1979 and 1980. Her monograph *The Chinese in Kula: A Farming Community in Old Hawaii* was commissioned by the Hawaii Chinese History Center in 1975, and her book *A Place Called Chinese America* (in collaboration with photographer Ginger Chih) was published by Kendall/ Hunt in 1982. Her poetry and articles have appeared in such publications as the *Bulletin of Concerned Asian Scholars, Third World Women, Montage: An Ethnic History of Women in Hawaii,* and *Breaking Silence: An Anthology of Contemporary Asian American Poets.*

Mark has a B.A. in Asian Studies and English from Mills College (Oakland, Ca.) and an M.A. in American Studies from the University of Hawaii, where she was also an East-West Center Communication Institute degree scholar. She currently resides in New York, where she is pursuing independent writing projects and working as Development Director for Asian CineVision, Inc., a media arts organization.